SCHOOL CHOICE IN CHILE

SCHOOL CHOICE IN CHILE

Two Decades of Educational Reform

VARUN GAURI

UNIVERSITY OF PITTSBURGH PRESS

Published by the University of Pittsburgh Press, Pittsburgh, Pa 15261
Copyright © 1998, University of Pittsburgh Press
All rights reserved
Manufactured in the United States of America
Printed on acid-free paper
10 9 8 7 6 5 4 3 2 1

Library of Congress Cataloging-in-Publication Data
Gauri, Varun, 1966–
       School choice in Chile : two decades of educational reform /
Varun Gauri.
       p. cm. — (Pitt Latin American series)
       Includes bibliographical references and index.

       ISBN 0-8229-4074-8 (cloth : acid-free paper)
       ISBN 0-8229-5678-0 (pbk. : acid-free paper)
       1. School choice—Chile.   2. Education and state—Chile.
3. Educational change—Chile.   I. Title.   II. Series.
       LB1027.9 .G38 1998
       379. 1 '11 '0983—ddc21   98-25322
                                                                        CIP

A CIP catalog record for this book is available from the
British Library.

CONTENTS

LIST OF TABLES

LIST OF ACRONYMS

AFPs	Pension Fund Managers
DEM	Municipal Department of Education
DIRPRES	Budget Office in the Ministry of Finance
DIRPROV	Provincial Directorate of the Ministry of Education
FCM	Municipal Common Fund
FIDE	Federation of Institutes of Education (a group of private schools)
LOCE	Constitutional Organic Law of Education
MECE	Program for the Improvement of the Equity and Quality of Education
ODEPLAN	National Planning Office
PADEM	Municipal Education Plan (sets teaching staff size)
PC	Communist Party
PDC	Christian Democratic Party
PER	Exam for the Assessment of School Achievement (standardized test)
PPD	Party for Democracy
PR	Radical Party
PS	Socialist Party
RN	National Renovation Party
SEREMI	Regional Secretariat of the Ministry of Education
SIMCE	System for the Measurement of the Quality of Education (standardized test)
SNED	National System for Performance Evaluation
SUBDERE	Subsecretariat for Regional Development of the Ministry of the Interior
UDI	Independent Democratic Union Party
USE	Educational Subventions Unit
UTM	Indexed Unit of Taxation

ACKNOWLEDGMENTS

A number of Chileans opened their homes and shared their days with me, offering afternoons and lively evenings without which my research would be a shadow of what it is. For stimulating conversation and the warmest hospitality, I want to thank Tomás Chuaqui and Paulina Rodríguez, Gina and Juan Pablo Manríquez, Carlos Inalaf and Paula Santandreu, Germán Quintana and Cecelia Acuña, Oscar Witke and Paula Ahumada, Oscar Espinoza, and Marichen Euler. An invitation from Francisco López provided professional accommodations and an active intellectual environment. I want to thank everyone at ILADES for their warmth and support of my project, and Osvaldo Larrañaga and Cristián Aedo for their collaboration. My debt to Chilean officials and educators is immense, too wide to enumerate here; but I especially want to thank two officials in the Ministry of Education, Cristián Cox and Sergio Nilo, who gave me encouragement and insight, and whose work ennobles the profession of government service.

This book profited greatly from the thoughtful advice, insightful comments, and patient assistance of Henry Bienen, Atul Kohli, Paul Sigmund, Jennifer Hochschild, Jeffrey Henig, Estelle James, Jeff Puryear, Carol Graham, Chris Paxson, Ilian Mihov, Ceci Rouse, Vijaya Ramachandran, and Germán Rodríguez. Sam Carlson and Julian Schweitzer first provided me with the opportunity to examine Chilean education. Grants from the National Science Foundation, the Center for International Studies of Princeton University, and the Compton Family Fund made the research possible. The views expressed here reflect neither the position of the Center for International Studies nor that of the World Bank.

I have wonderful friends whose high spirits have helped to carry this project to completion. For their thoughts, conversation, and friendship, I want to thank Kateri Carmola, David Neidorf, David Rocah, Sarah Kass Mandelbaum, Dan Coleman, Jeff Edelstein, Mark Paul, Zhenya Erlij, Charlotte Ellertson, Brian Kux, Naomi Rood, Daniel Goldberg, Peter Cannavo, Greg Felker, Janmejaya Sinha, Ayesha Khan, Wendy Blattner, and Tom Inck. In dedicating this work to my brother, Vinny Gauri, and to my parents, Kul and Kamlesh Gauri, I celebrate the love and joy they take in me, and I in them.

The Contemporary Movement to Reform the Social Sectors

Without being too literal about it, we think
reformers would do well to entertain the notion
that choice *is* a panacea.

CHUBB AND MOE, *Politics, Markets, and America's Schools*

This book examines the argument that the introduction of market mechanisms in the supply of and demand for schools will by itself enhance educational performance. It analyzes the microeconomic assumptions underlying the proposition that elementary and secondary education *could* function as a market. But because in policy so much depends on how plans are implemented and on how programs become embedded in particular institutions, the method is not only an examination of the principles of and theoretical arguments for school choice but is primarily an assessment of what is perhaps the world's most ambitious attempt to design and implement a program of educational choice: Chile's reforms of 1980.

Under General Pinochet's military regime, Chile adopted free-market principles in most industries and services, including elementary and secondary education. The regime transferred all public schools, which the Ministry of Education had managed from Santiago, to the municipalities; and it started financing the operation of all tuition-free private schools, whether

1

philanthropic or for-profit, at exactly the same level as the newly municipalized schools. Those policies resulted in the creation of about one thousand new private schools in ten years, a dramatic result for a country that had a total of about ten thousand public and private schools in 1990. Enrollments in the private subsidized elementary schools grew from about 306,000 in 1980 (a 14 percent share) to over 610,000 in 1988 (a 30 percent share). All of that gain came at the expense of municipal schools, which were losing in the competition for students. At the secondary level, enrollments in private subsidized schools grew from 38,000 in 1980 (a 7 percent share) to over 269,00 in 1988 (a 37 percent share). In 1996, essentially tuition-free private subsidized schools accounted for about 35 percent of total national enrollments (including the 2 percent in schools that private industry groups directed), municipal schools for 57 percent, and unsubsidized, expensive, private schools for 8 percent. In the capital city of Santiago, home to about one-third of Chile's fourteen million inhabitants, private schools of all types together accounted for over 55 percent of enrollments.

Despite disagreements with several of the military regime's education policies, Chile's democratic government that took office in 1990 for the most part stayed the course. Consequently, Chilean education continues to approximate a national choice model more closely than any other system in the world. Although the central government finances the operation of more than 90 percent of the approximately 11,600 educational establishments in the nation, it manages none of them. Municipal and private subsidized schools receive equal funding on the basis of a monthly attendance-based subsidy called the "subvention." Since parents can enroll their students in any school that will accept them, the subvention functions like a voucher in the subsidized sectors: a government payment follows each student to the school of his or her choice. As a result of the funding mechanism and the economies of scale, municipalities and private schools compete for student enrollment share. While the central government prescribes a curriculum for schools that do not develop their own, sets standards for school infrastructure, and supervises school operations, the municipalities and private schools possess the liberty to make personnel decisions, operate schools, and establish their own school policies, including innovations in curriculum and governance that they believe will make them more attractive to their clients.

After more than a decade of school choice, several measures of the performance of the Chilean educational system seem to have improved. The population as a whole is more educated, the elementary school drop-out rate has fallen sharply, and gross enrollment in secondary schools increased from

65 percent in 1980 to nearly 80 percent in 1996. Most famousl·
economy recovered vigorously after the deep recession of th·
and by 1997 its economy had experienced fourteen years of
expanding at an average rate of 6.6 percent per annum over that pc..·
remaining generally unaffected by currency and financial shocks that struck
the rest of Latin America. Chile's economic performance lends a glow to all
of its policies, including those in education, and in the circles of international policy making Chile's economic, political, and social reforms can
indeed possess the aura of a panacea.

Still, within Chile the repression of the military regime made its policies
controversial; and many societal groups, particularly teachers, are unhappy
with the educational reforms. They believe that the commercialization of
schooling can jeopardize the integrity of education, that turmoil and
turnover hinder educational goals, and that the ministry and the new private
school owners cannot be trusted. Stories such as the following from Claudia,
a Spanish teacher at a small private subsidized school, recounted in March
1990, surfaced even during the repressive period of the military regime:

> I didn't stay on [at the school] because they changed owners.
> When I joined there were great teachers, it was great, it was infor-
> mal, you made a circle of friends just like that; but the next year
> they changed owners and the whole thing became just commercial.
> . . . I failed some students, which wasn't a surprise, but when at
> the end of the semester I went to collect the notebooks, everyone I
> failed had passed the course; in other words, they had changed my
> grades. And they explained to me that the idea was not to lose stu-
> dents—if one failed them during the first semester they would
> leave. So it was better to fail them second year, because then a kid
> already has a year under his belt and he's unlikely to leave. . . . So
> no, I wasn't going to do that. No, no more. (Gysling 1992, 103)

At the same time, many Chileans believe passionately in the education
reforms, arguing that they are effective, fair, and fundamentally moral. For
them, the criticisms of teachers like Claudia are the predictable and reflexive
response of union members whose job security is threatened. Touting the
strong supply response of the private sector to the new subsidies that did not
discriminate between public and private schools, an analyst with a right-of-
center think tank in Santiago cited findings that impressed Chileans and
international policy experts alike:

School children in Santiago. Courtesy of the Economic Development Institute of the World Bank.

> In 1982, 75 percent of students attended municipal or central schools under control of the Ministry of Education. Currently that percentage has fallen to about 58 percent. The school population has been gradually moving to private schools, whether purely private, subsidized, or belonging to industry groups. The explanation for this tendency has to do with the greater confidence that parents have been placing in private education, whether purely private or subsidized, because that type of school has higher test scores. (Libertad y Desarrollo 1994, 25)

In fact, the origins of the Chilean education reforms owe as much to the long history of conflicts between liberals and conservatives in Chile regarding the appropriate role for the state in education as they do to applied microeconomics. By treating public and private schools equally, the new system guarantees the freedom of parents to educate their children as they wish, argue proponents. Senator José Piñera, a leading architect of the military regime's labor and social policies, expressed a view widely held among Pinochet's supporters, who constituted 45 percent of the Chilean electorate

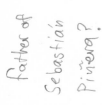

Father of Sebastián Piñera?

in 1988 and remain sizable and vocal, when he enumerated the educational principles of his political party, the right-of-center Renovación Nacional (RN):

> [The educational goals of our party are] first, to protect and safeguard educational liberties; second, to be consistent in the application of the subsidiarity of the state in educational matters, which means that in this area the state has more obligations than rights; and third, to recognize with complete clarity the existence of sectors that actively participate in education—the municipal and the private subsidized. We put forth the fundamental idea that the treatment of both has to be equitable, in such a manner that the equality of opportunity is applied not only to students but also to the institutions that provide education. (*Historia de Ley* 1992, 4956)

But Chile does not possess the social, political, and economic resources necessary to implement deep educational reforms with relative ease. In 1989, about 40 percent of Chileans were living in poverty, a large part of them in the informal economy. How were individuals who were excluded from mainstream society to become sophisticated consumers of education? How long would it take? For many of the critics of the Chilean reforms, such as Isabel, an elementary school teacher in Santiago, the novelties in the educational reforms were mostly propaganda, while the fundamental needs of the children remain unsatisfied:

> The curricula are still governed by the Ministry of Education. But it is true [now that the municipality is in charge] we have to celebrate the day of so-and-so and the day of whoever, Joe Schmoe's day, and we have to put on a three-ring circus, with a parade and everything else. They want the community to look the best, to be the best dressed; but you know the poor kids are dying of hunger. I mean, they present an image that's not true. . . . There's a lot of stuff for outsiders and not much that's left for the kids. This was my big fight in my school. You were there having class and the kids had to run out to prepare for an athletic review. You were having classes and they came to get you to prepare for chorus. You were having classes and they came to get you for a thousand differ-

ent things. They used to say that the school had to look good, had to be the best and the most thriving. I said in the Council that we lost a lot of time on things that had nothing to do with the school. But according to the director, all this was part of the "holistic training of the children." (Edwards et al. 1991, 90)

This book evaluates Isabel's point that nothing fundamental changed in the new Chilean system. It also examines the evidence that students in Chilean private schools perform better on test scores, the historical context for Senator Piñera's claim that private schools have a right to equal treatment, and Claudia's vivid description of commercialism in Chilean schools. It will offer answers to the following questions. Has overall educational performance improved in the new system? Do parents in Chile choose the best schools for their children, and do they know which schools are best? How do schools choose among eligible students? And how did the teachers' union press its case, first in an authoritarian setting and then in Chile's highly centralized political party system?

Before proceeding with the analysis, however, it is worth reflecting on what is at issue. The Chilean educational reforms are representative of a broad international movement to introduce market forces into social sector service delivery. A study of them illuminates the political dynamics and the policy relevance of those reforms in Latin America and throughout the world.

Education and Health in the Washington Consensus

While the 1980s are remembered as a difficult and divisive period in Latin America and much of the developing world, a "lost decade" and the "decade of debt," the 1990s have been a decade of rebuilding. Seemingly, developing country civilian leaders, their electorates, and Washington policy elites all agree that democratization, markets, and marketlike state institutions are essential for growth and well-being (Williamson 1990). After a period in which hyperinflation and economic stagnation forced regimes to focus almost exclusively on programs of macroeconomic stabilization and structural adjustment, developing nations are again concerned with the broad complex of goals called development, including growth, the eradication of poverty, and institution building. Rebuilding strategies emphasize factors long held to be important by conservatives, such as free elections, the modernization of the state, reductions in tariffs and other barriers to inter-

national trade, and the liberalization of financial markets, as wel
new and center-left objectives, such as ecological preservation
milial justice.[1] Nearly all Latin American countries have moved
petitive elections and freer markets. Although it remains to be
this "model" for the political economy will be able to manage or over...
the class, ethnic, and other divisions that persist in Latin America, some
believe that it represents not only a consensus but an epochal turning point
in the understanding of state-market relations, the ideological "end of history" (Waggman 1994).

Some of the rebuilding strategies have received sustained attention in the
literature. The transitions to democracy from authoritarian rule, in particular, as well as the politics of macroeconomic adjustment and the privatization
of state industries are now well-defined areas of disciplinary interest. Less
studied, indeed sometimes barely noticed, is a major reconceptualization of
social policy underway in these countries. Most of their modernization programs involve decentralization and privatization in the social sectors in a
manner that threatens the state's traditional roles in health care, education,
social security, and other spheres. The welfare state is being reorganized and,
in conceptual terms, perhaps dismantled. Although governments are implementing these experiments unevenly, in start and stop fashion as political
conditions permit, the idea that social service ministries can and should
behave like firms is gaining increasing acceptance. Where the proposals have
been carried through, the central governments have in some cases decentralized responsibilities to provincial or municipal authorities; at other times the
services are privatized outright.

Decentralization and privatization are not in themselves novel processes,
of course. Large countries have long opted for federated state systems out of
necessity, and their provincial or local bodies have in the past assumed
responsibility for social service delivery.[2] Some of the current privatization
and decentralization strategies constitute a similarly "common sense"
response to the rapid growth of urban populations. As more and more families move to Latin American cities, the demands on health and education
ministries become more intense and social services grow in volume and com-
plexity. It is becoming logistically difficult for officials in one locale to
administer a large, interrelated system. It is time-consuming and unnecessary, for example, for ministries of education to issue a check for each acqui-
sition in every school in the country.

But the movement to revamp the welfare state, though it shares an inter-

, with the common sense motive, moves beyond it. Both types of reform ook to manage service delivery more effectively, and they both seek efficiency gains from reorganization. The contemporary reforms are distinct, however, to the extent that they advocate decentralization or privatization even in cases where it would appear counterintuitive or against common sense: when local capacity is relatively underdeveloped, for example, or when service clientele are not accustomed to behaving like consumers. Ideologically driven reforms not only decentralize service delivery but, in transferring responsibilities to localities or private agents, reconceive the long-standing idea of an entitlement to social services. A number of countries have recently initiated or proposed dramatic changes in this direction, forming, with the general support these reforms enjoy in the international lending institutions, a wave of post-welfare thinking for the social sectors.[3]

Put simply, the ideological movement for privatizing social delivery believes that social ministries are firms involved in the production of goods. Because service providers generally are not funded on the basis of the goods provided, the services need not reflect preferences of the service users, and providers have no incentive to provide high-quality goods. The incentives for providers in the social sector ministries must be restructured, or so goes the argument. An influential development economist writes:

> IBM has just about the same number of people on its payroll as Venezuela's Ministry of Education, but it faces competitive product and input markets and a highly exacting capital and financial market. These markets send signals that force the organization to change, often in quite a radical manner. The centralized and public provision of health and education services implies quite a different structure. Production units—e.g., hospitals and schools—receive resources through a budget independently of the quality or quantity of output. These budgets can hardly be adjusted to meet changes in demand, be it between different medical services in a given hospital or between different school districts. (Hausmann 1994)

Centralized production systems lead not only to a failure to respond to changes in demand, argue the post-welfare reformers, but to excessive politicization as provider groups, such as teachers' and doctors' unions, capture the systems of service delivery. Excessive personnel costs and allocative inefficiencies are unavoidable when the distribution systems emphasize political objectives. An Argentinean policy analyst argues that because various governmental bureaucracies often provide duplicate services in health care and social security, "investments in technology, infrastructure development and utilization of human resources may have a sectoral rationality but bring about a global inefficiency due to the ill-use of expensive medical resources." This analyst contends that political objectives push up administrative costs, citing the fact that in Nicaragua, Honduras, the Dominican Republic, Venezuela, and Mexico, "administrative expenditure in the field of social security represents over 20 percent of the total expenditure" (Isuani 1994).

The idea of state modernization in the social sector has also won over politicians and analysts from the political Center and Left, who in general are less impressed with the conclusions of public choice theory than with the democratic resonances of decentralization. They believe that decentralization allows more citizen participation in the state, and in precisely those services that most concern marginalized populations. A UN official leading state reform in Carácas believes that "true participation is far more possible in the framework of decentralized social programs. In such instances, programs are taken to a community unit and this provides an arena for joint work between the people in charge of the programs and the community, for a dynamic exchange of ideas in horizontal conditions" (Kliksberg 1994).

The movement thrives, like any policy program, on specific, immediate political and economic motives and circumstances. Most countries in Latin America are emerging from, or indeed still struggling with, macroeconomic instability, long-term debt service, and fiscal cutbacks. In this context, large increases in social service spending do not appear likely in the short to medium term. Focusing on improved service delivery and efficiency is a way to meet political pressure for services without having to "throw money at the problem." It is also apparent to policy makers that social sector enhancement is required to make structural adjustment politically palatable. Public sector employees experienced declining wages and rising unemployment during the adjustment programs of the last decade, and morale and service quality have deteriorated in many countries. Political consolidation of the adjustment programs and models, however, requires an improvement in the quality of services: popular sectors must see gains from the sacrifice in the short term. While this suggests the political value of social safety nets, emergency social funds, and public employment programs in protecting vulnerable groups during the adjustment process (Graham 1994), it also implies the need for governments to demonstrate a commitment to improving social services over the medium term. In the context of budgetary and macroeconomic limits and key political concessions, such as "understandings" concerning defense spending, squeezing efficiency gains out of the system appears to be the only alternative (Angell and Graham 1995). Efficiency gains from improved social sector services might in turn lead to equity enhancements, a fact that explains the moral energy of some of the neoliberal reformers, like those in Chile.

The movement to reorganize the welfare state also exploits a specific political context. For the anticommunist military regimes, of which Pinochet's Chile is the best example, privatizing social sector services was an instrument to break the grip of public sector unions, and their allegedly socialist leaders, on the social ministries. For regimes that are not virulently anticommunist but still conservative, modernization in the sector can be a form of "load shedding": when they transfer responsibilities to local agents without a requisite transfer in resources, they rid themselves of a burdensome task as well as the political responsibility for its shortcomings (Feigenbaum and Henig 1994). Finally, any contemporary regime might view the intro-duction of market forces in the social sector as a primarily destructive instru-ment: in Touraine's language, the market economy is "the absolute weapon against the mobilising state and the totalitarian state." In this view, the wide-spread movement toward market organization is best seen not as the con-struction of a new order but as the destruction of the old neocorporatist order, the social sector configuration that dominated Latin America for the past fifty years and in which unions and industry groups allied with the state and mobilized for the sake of mutual benefit. Touraine writes:

> The main error in defining the current situation as the tri-
> umph of the liberal solution is to confuse two operations that his-
> tory, on the contrary, differentiates: the destruction of the old sys-
> tem and the building of the new. . . . The former has to be
> destroyed first, along with all of the forms of its hold on society.
> Today, the only known means of doing this efficiently is to imple-
> ment the market economy, for it is much less a positive principle
> of economic and social organization than a weapon against politi-
> cal, ideological or bureaucratic control of the economy. (Touraine
> 1994, 50)

The Significance of the Chilean Story

Chilean political and economic institutions are noteworthy in Latin America for their relative soundness, efficiency, and honesty. Their resurgence in the late 1980s was as impressive as their collapse in the 1970s was dramatic. For some analysts, including members of the governmental and multilateral agencies that constitute the "Washington consensus," Chilean institutions might be not only noteworthy but paradigmatic. Chile has seemingly resolved the cyclical conflicts between ideological populism and conservatism that have plagued Latin America and has moved to a political accommodation between civilian leaders and the military, between statists and free marketeers, and among Christian Democrats, Socialists, and conservatives, that allows for both long-term low inflation growth and openly contested elections. If it manages to reverse the increase in inequality that accompanied the growth of the 1980s and to attack the problem of social, political, and economic marginalization, its political-economic path, as well as the particular choices its leaders have made, might well be something of a model for other Latin American countries. Touraine observes:

> [A] close watch must be kept on the Chilean example. With a strong capacity for state action, the reinforcement of enterprise, a recent recovery in the rate of union membership, an active social policy that has reduced the proportion of poor people from 40 to 32 per cent of the total population—perhaps even less—Chile today meets all the conditions of development and will soon become a truly developing country if it strengthens its entrepreneurial capacity and if it speeds up its policy of social and economic reintegration of the underprivileged sectors. (Touraine 1994, 61)

Chile's reform of the financing and delivery of government services in the late 1970s and early 1980s constitutes the developing world's exemplary case of contemporary state modernization, decentralization, and privatization. Ideologically inspired, the military regime's technocrats restructured the labor market, introduced vouchers into public housing programs, legalized private health insurance while adding market elements to the public health system, turned over most of the social security system to private pension fund managers (AFPs), transferred the management of schools and primary health clinics to municipalities, strengthened the municipal finance system, and created a voucherlike mechanism to finance both public and private schools. The democratic government has committed itself to deepening, democratizing, and enriching the military regime's social sector policies.

Education is an interesting and analytically useful sector for the study of the post-welfare model because its "industrial organization" apparently violates central presuppositions of microeconomics. Specifically, schoolchildren are less "rational" than ideal consumers, the educational good is not homogeneous because the definition of school quality remains controversial, the search costs for information about educational products and prices are high, the transaction cost of changing schools is difficult to measure, factor inputs in the form of teachers are not perfectly interchangeable, and the positive externalities from schooling, though universally acknowledged to be high, are so widespread as to be nearly inestimable. For many of these reasons, enlightenment liberals of the last century advocated and succeeded in creating government-managed, national systems of education. The post-welfare model acknowledges market failures in education—indeed, even the purest neoliberals advocate continued government funding for education on the grounds that it is a public good—but they believe that welfare losses from central government management are now too great to justify continued centralization.

An examination of the sector will help to illuminate their position, both for education and for their broader post-welfare claims. This study reviews the Chilean reforms in detail in light of public choice theory and arguments for educational choice, and it uncovers a series of policy problems that have undermined the functioning of the Chilean system (chapter 2). It argues that these difficulties pose obstacles not only for Chilean education but for the use of post-welfare incentive structures in the social sectors. The study then reviews existing evidence regarding the Chilean reforms, presents data from an original survey of 726 households in greater Santiago, and develops a model for the factors that contribute to search success in the Chilean choice system (see chapter 3). It concedes that determining whether the post-welfare incentives increase inequality, as critics charge, will require more comparative work, but it establishes benchmark data for comparison and discovers problems related to selection in the Chilean system. The study then examines the politics of reform in Chilean education both in the military and democratic governments, arguing that although autonomy from interest groups permitted the military regime to impose the reforms, the secrecy and isolation it required prevented the conditions necessary for their consolidation; and that the democratic government's efforts stumbled against the influence of the teachers' union (chapter 4). Finally, the conclusion presents the implications of the study for policy, and it explores the structural factors intrinsic to education that prevent a simple application of post-welfare reforms (chapter 5).

Before we begin, two points of clarification should be noted. First, *post-welfare* is a term of art appropriated for this research. It refers to the use of any incentive structures in the delivery of social sector services that seek to mimic those of an ideal market, including vouchers, merit pay, municipal taxation powers, user fees, and the like. The justification for grouping these diverse instruments together under one label is political: their currency and use in the contemporary policy climate seem to be correlated with another. Second, this study focuses exclusively on those aspects of the Chilean education reforms that are relevant to the use of post-welfare incentives. A number of other initiatives, including revisions of curricular content, the ministry's program targeted at the poorest schools in the country (Programa P-900), the (once) World Bank–financed project of institutional fortification and renewal (Programa de Mejoramiento de la Equidad y Calidad de la Educación, or MECE), the effort to connect all schools to the Internet (La Red Enlaces), and President Frei's plan to lengthen the school day and promote teacher training, though very important for the future of Chilean education, are not considered.

The Theory and Practice of School Choice in Chile

The Teaching State

An examination of the history of Chilean education and its tradition of centralism makes clear the near revolutionary status of the post-welfare reforms. In Chile education has been and is an essential and constitutional function of a unitary state. The government has trained teachers, managed schools, and financed basic education since the middle of the last century, shortly after the state's consolidation following independence. For most of the twentieth century, Chileans joined in near consensus agreement on the importance of the state's educative role, a doctrine they called the *estado docente,* or the "teaching state."

With the French model as inspiration, the Chilean educational system had been conceived so that its minister could say, like his famous and hoary French counterpart, that on a given day at a given time all students were reading a determined page in Virgil.[1] The founders of the state's University of Chile designed it to manage or supervise every school in the country. From its creation in 1842 the university assumed the authority to grant all valid educational certificates in the nation and to train and license all teachers and university professors. State education in Chile expanded steadily in

the nineteenth century, with free primary schools opened in every department in 1860, the adoption of the German concentric model of learning and
new primary schools in 1883, and the founding of the Pedagogical Institute,
where six imported German teachers (only one of whom spoke Spanish)
began to train Chilean *liceo* instructors, in 1889. There was a brief interlude
from 1872 to 1875 when a Conservative government under the banner of
"educational freedom" for religious families, *la libertad de enseñanza,* allowed
private schools to grant certificates without state inspection; but on the
whole the Liberals and positivists succeeded in widening and standardizing
education in the name of Reason. By the turn of the century, "Chile had a
centralist and bureaucratically organized educational system, with an increasingly professionalized teaching corps in both its primary and secondary level"
(Cox 1984, 52). The state controlled the entire educational system, and its
enrollment constituted about three-fourths of all students in basic and secondary schools in 1900.

As the Radical Party and the middle class grew in strength in the early
part of the twentieth century, the body of teachers became an important element in that coalition. Teacher leaders began to receive important jobs in the
ministry and began to expect to be consulted by political leaders. In some
sense the teachers became the ministry and the ministry the teachers,
although there were significant class and power divisions between elementary
school teachers and those at higher levels of education (Núñez 1986). Some
of these divisions spurred the creation of coalitions to democratize and
decentralize educational organization, such as the proposals of Darío Salas
around 1917, the reform of the Teachers' Association of 1927, the Experimental Plan of San Carlos of 1928, and the Arica Plan of 1961; but centralized state control of education was never seriously questioned.[2] A teacher,
Pedro Aguirre Cerda, became president in 1938. The ideology (and the social
organization in which it was embedded) re-expressed itself as the develop-
mentalist educational planning models of the 1950s and 1960s, which
designed a school supply expansion under the Christian Democrats that
eventually led to near-universal primary education. Chilean education
became the envy of Latin America. By the late 1960s, the ministry owned
and managed schools for over two million elementary and secondary school
students, employed over 70,000 tenured civil servants, trained and recruited
them all through its normal schools, provided medical care for its employees,
ran a half-dozen related institutions, and, of course, approved every degree
and every class in the nation.[3]

In the crucial years of the late nineteenth century, the *estado docente* had

had two groups of detractors. On the one hand Conservatives and Catholics had opposed the education of peasants and resented its encroachment on the traditionally religious task of education; and on the other, laissez-faire economists, or "free traders" (*librecambistas*), argued that government ought to leave education to the laws of supply and demand. The Liberal positivist intellectuals charged the Catholics with elitism and superstition and the economists with misrepresenting the essentially public character of education (Fogg 1978). The Liberal positivists argued that a secular, enlightened state had an obligation to pay for and manage a nonsectarian, public system of education for the purpose of elevating the national culture and spreading scientific truths. Arguing against the economists, Valentín Letelier, the leading Chilean positivist, made some interesting comments on information asymmetries and public goods as early as 1885:

> But education is not born, nor does it live and develop, in the conditions in which other industries are established, are built, and prosper; and although that individual who knows about the commodities he needs can choose effectively between one good and another, an individual without any instruction lacks the competence to choose between one education and another. . . .
>
>   In public administration most nations follow an almost invariable rule: when the state provides personal services (transport of passengers, cargo, telegrams, disinfection of dwellings, etc.), it charges the persons who directly benefit; when it provides general services (disinfection of cities, public order, public lighting, etc.), it supports them with general contributions. Now, while special instruction is a personal service, aimed in fact at a small portion of citizens and whose benefits are enjoyed principally by those who receive it, general instruction is a social service aimed at everyone without exception and whose benefits translate less in the private advantage of the individuals who receive it than in the diffusion and elevation of national culture. (Letelier 1927, 42, 104)

Intellectual descendants of the two original opponents of the *estado docente,* Catholics and classical economists, came together in a historical alliance after 1973. For its own purposes, the military junta supported them; and the years from 1973 to 1989 witnessed a determined effort to liquidate the political, social, and intellectual structures that had built and sustained the *estado docente.* The following section examines the theoretical arguments that informed the neoliberal reforms in Chile and that continue to influence the movement to transform the social sectors around the world.

Public Choice, Decentralization, and Educational Choice

The theoretical foundations of post-welfare service delivery are at least as old as Adam Smith, who in 1776 argued that "in modern times, the diligence of public teachers is more or less corrupted by the circumstances, which render them more or less independent of their success and reputation" (Smith 1976, 5: 300). The idea, here applied specifically to education, was that the allocation of goods and services by the sovereign resulted in an outcome that would be, both in terms of absolute magnitude and intrasectoral distribution, economically irrational. Distributing goods via the market, on the other hand, would give recipients the opportunity to choose what they like and compel them to pay for their choices directly, a system rewarding only those providers who satisfied their demands and imposing limits on budgetary expenditures.

A teacher helps two students in a one-room schoolhouse in southern Chile. Courtesy of the Economic Development Institute of the World Bank.

In the 1960s and 1970s, public choice theory rediscovered and elaborated that simple principle of classical economics, and although public choice literature is now vast and specialized, its core argument remains straightforward. While the public at large bears the costs of taxation, particular lobbies benefit from governmental concessions and spending; and because the costs of organizing are much lower for smaller groups than for larger ones, these lobbies obtain tax breaks and programs at the expense of the larger groups of taxpayers and service recipients, for whom collective action is much more difficult to achieve (Olson 1965; Hardin 1982). The result is a tendency for government deficits to balloon and for the provision of goods and services to be ill-matched to recipients' needs (Buchanan and Wagner 1977). While the private sector seeks to eliminate potential lethargy and rent-seeking behavior in its executives with stock options and other incentive packages, no such incentive structures tie public sector managers to the "owners" of government, leaving them susceptible to interest group influence and to simple lassitude (Buchanan, Tollison, and Tullock 1980). As a result, businesses also innovate more than governments. A second problem, the existence of inefficient intrasectoral allocations, follows from the fact that political negotiation does not employ a divisible currency, and like any barter economy it achieves Pareto-optimal outcomes only with great difficulty (Buchanan 1968; Musgrave 1959).[4]

Historical tradition and public values other than efficiency, such as justice and equality, make the logical implication of public choice theory—abolishing governmental ministries and letting the market respond to needs wherever it reasonably can—undesirable. Institutional economists point out that government agencies also reduce the informational and transaction costs of pure market exchanges (Ostrom, Feeny, and Picht 1988; E. Ostrom 1990), and microeconomists have long noted that externalities might lead to the under- or over-financing of a given good or service if left to the private sector alone. Rather, public choice theory would have the government limit its role to correcting market imperfections, or to providing services according to allocative principles that mirror those of the market. In the latter case, purchasing agents, whether actual consumers, local governments, or some other autonomous bodies, would make informed choices about their preferences and needs and pay directly the cost of the goods or services purchased. Productive agents, whether independent contractors, private for-profit service providers, or even local governments, would compete with each other for "customers" and purchase inputs at real cost (Ostrom and Ostrom 1977). A "principle of fiscal equivalence," in which those who benefit from a service are also those who pay its costs, would prevail in the public economy to the extent possible, with governmental tax credits or subsidies targeted exclusively to the poor (Olson 1969; Oates 1972; Bahl and Linn 1992). The central government would finance the redistributive programs because municipal redistribution causes outmigration of wealthy residents, leading to the erosion of local tax bases (Peterson 1981). In this model, the monopoly power of traditional providers would give way to competition in the provision of goods and services.

The theory's specific institutional recommendations for the delivery of public goods depend on the particular traits of the sector in question. Those traits include the degree to which the provision of the public good is excludable, the extent to which its quality or performance level is measurable, and the degree to which its use or consumption is joint or subtractable. If the providers' performance is difficult to measure, as it is in education, purchasing agents will find it hard to contract out a service because the contract will be difficult to write and monitor. Or if the benefits of a public good are not excludable, as in the benefits of widespread immunization, user fees on service recipients would be inefficient. The theory would require a detailed examination of the sector and its "industrial organization" before prescribing improvements (Savas 1987).

Although public choice theory developed the intellectual foundations of post-welfare thinking, management studies relying on it are now at least as influential. The notions that service recipients are customers whose voices and preferences must be heard, that competition among providers is better for service quality than centralized provision, that decentralization fosters community participation, and that incentives work best when agencies fund outcomes and not inputs are central elements in currently influential management movements such as "Reinventing Government" and "Total Quality Management" (Osborne and Gaebler 1992; Carr and Littman 1993). The texts and ideas of the movements, however, tend to be less self-conscious of the conditions necessary for proposed reforms to be efficiency-improving than public choice theory; and their conclusions are all too often accepted uncritically, without testing their assumptions against the prevailing political and social environment where the reforms are to be implemented. This chapter illustrates this problem for the Chilean educational post-welfare reforms in detail.

In the development literature, the most common guises for public choice theory are the arguments supporting the decentralization and privatization of public enterprises and services (Bennett 1990; Bennett 1994;

Ostrom, Schroeder, and Wynne 1993). Decentralizing decision making and regulative power, taxation authority, and budgetary control to provincial or municipal governments permits a tighter fit between voters' preferences and the services governments provide because preferences for services and tax rates are presumably more homogenous locally than nationally. In addition, local decision making allows governments to exploit local comparative advantages in the production of goods and services and to attract other residents with similar preferences. In public choice theory, then, unlike political and legal analysis, decentralization is continuous with privatization: the latter is merely the extension of decision-making, taxative, and budgetary power further down the line, to the production units themselves, which are schools in education and clinics or hospitals in the case of health care. Decentralized productive agents levy taxes in the form of user fees or prices, exercise budgetary discretion through their input choices, and respond to voter preferences on the basis of exit signals. Elections and referenda are then understood to be the political simulacra of the direct expression of preferences and choices. The perfectly functioning market, because it permits the unmediated expression of those preferences, is sometimes described as more "democratic" than democratic politics.

Decentralization and privatization in the social sector take a variety of forms. Decentralization can involve the transfer of administrative responsibility to local branches of government ministries, the delegation of managerial authority to semiautonomous or parastatal organizations, or the transfer of managerial, technical, and financial authority to autonomous local governments. The last, empowering autonomous local governments, is the strongest form; and some writers reserve the term *decentralization* for it alone, preferring *deconcentration* and *delegation* for the first two forms of transfer.[5] Because local governments are relatively weak and underdeveloped throughout Latin America and elsewhere in the developing world, the decentralization of social services often requires previously having strengthened the legal, financial, and managerial powers of the municipalities and provinces. The privatization of social service delivery also takes a variety of forms, each of which is usually based on one or more combinations of the sale or transfer of state assets to the private sector (as in the sale of a water treatment facility), contracting private companies to provide specified services (as when cities hire private sanitation companies to remove waste or when national governments contract with health maintenance organizations to care for indigent populations), and the use of vouchers to pay providers on the basis of consumer preferences (such as when individuals purchase groceries with food stamps).[6] When social services are thought to be public goods, as in education and health, the theory has the state continue to finance their provision even if the private sector assumes responsibility for their delivery and management.

Post-welfare writers often portray education as a particularly egregious example of the problems to which centralized service provision is liable. Educational systems are represented as labyrinthine and self-serving organizations (or even "Kremlinesque"), teachers and principals as tenured functionaries with no incentive to perform well, and children and families as passive victims in a system captured by and for the bureaucrats. The widespread use of the educational example in the field of public choice is due in part to the influence of Friedman's famous article of 1955, in which he argued, as part of a broader claim about the role of government in service provision, that the existence of externalities in the education sector justifies governmental funding but not the governmental management of schools. He proposed replacing public schools with direct subsidies to demand in the form of education vouchers. Like Smith, Friedman was primarily concerned with the problem of incentives for government workers:

> With respect to teachers' salaries, the major problem is not that they are too low on the average—they may well be too high on the average—but that they are too uniform and rigid. Poor teachers are grossly overpaid and good teachers grossly underpaid. . . . In any bureaucratic, essentially civil-service organization, standard salary scales are almost inevitable; it is next to impossible to simulate competition capable of providing wide differences in salaries according to merit. The educators, which means the teachers themselves, come to exercise primary control. The parent or local community comes to exercise little control. (Friedman 1955, 1962)

Control is central to the influential movement for vouchers and "educational choice" in the United States. It is argued that parents have a moral if not legal right to control the education of their children, and that this right extends to the liberty to choose a school without having to incur the tax "penalty" now charged to families of private school students (Coons and Sugarman 1978). Other proponents of "choice" concede that the state's responsibility to control the education of children is legitimate but that this responsibility ought to be shared with parents. In settings without any competition, however, which is the case in U.S. urban environments, the state's power becomes monopolistic, eliminating the critical and salutary role that communities and families ought to play in education (Peterson 1990). Where educational systems resemble monopolies, the incentives for curricular innovation disappear, and parental participation in schools declines. Participation permits the match between school values and family values believed to be critical for learning (Comer 1989).

The most influential theory of educational "choice" argues that control is crucial for effective schools (Chubb and Moe 1990). The writers contend that democratic politics leads interest groups to consolidate their electoral winnings in the form of bureaucratic rules that limit the discretion of future electoral winners who might reverse their gains. These rules, though politically rational, obviate the elements of school organization that countless studies have shown to be the most effective for learning: principals with wide discretion, coherent and clear goals, and well-structured organization (Rutter 1979; Sizer 1984). Private schools, it is argued, are more likely to exhibit the organization characteristic of effective schools, and a voucher system would provide the institutional environment most conducive to the establishment of effective schools.[7]

A variety of arguments, then, support the use of market forces in the public sector. Instituting one of the most radical free market experiments ever attempted, the policy makers who designed the Chilean educational reforms used many of those concepts explicitly. The next section describes the legal framework for the military regime's modernization.

The Legal Framework for the Chilean Reforms

Arguably the "most profound transformation ever experienced in Chilean public education" was an idea conceived, designed, and implemented in about eighteen months (Infante and Schiefelbein 1992, 4). There exists no comprehensive narrative of the events leading to the decision, nor, given the paucity of remaining documents, is one likely to be written. One account refers to a meeting in the house of Education Minister Alfredo Prieto in January 1980 as the moment of "definitive decision": those attending moved to go ahead with the "municipalization" of all state schools as soon as possible (Espinoza and González 1993, 114). But given the personalized and secretive policy making of the military regime, in the absence of votes and clear procedures, it is impossible to know what was definitive and what provisional. Even the participants did not know the extent of their own authority, whether their decisions were reversible or not.

It is clear that from mid-1979 to late 1980 the handful of University of Chicago school economists who headed social sector policy making in the military government—including Finance Minister Sergio de Castro, Director of Budget Juan Carlos Méndez, and Chief of the Planning Office (ODE-PLAN) Miguel Kast—explored how to "modernize" education. They considered varying combinations of educational decentralization and privatization and concluded that the state was not ready for an outright sale or transfer of schools and universities to the private sector although (it is rumored) some economists did forward a textbook application of Friedman's voucher proposal. Méndez, after taking a trip to examine the educational system of Belgium and after discussing various proposals with Kast, Castro, and others, defended municipalization before the junta. According to Méndez, junta members Leigh, Merino, and Mendosa were skeptical; but Pinochet supported it strongly, and his opinion was, of course, decisive.[8]

The Law of Municipal Revenues of 1979 served as the legal foundation for the transfer of schools and primary health clinics to municipalities. In Article 38 it declared a new municipal prerogative: "[Municipalities] can also assume control of services that are being provided by public or private sector entities, remaining subject to the principle of *subsidiariedad*" in the latter case; and can of their own accord finance works of community improvement" (Decreto Ley No. 3603, Artículo 38, December 24, 1979).

Although appearing to advocate optional and locally evaluated decisions, the reference to assuming "control of services" justified a centrally mandated system of municipal education. Municipal mayors, or alcaldes, most of whom were military officers, were ordered to assume control of educational services even in the regions where if a municipal government had possessed the capacity to measure the efficiency gains of local school management it would have declined to do so.

Three additional pieces of legislation completed the basic legal framework for the new system. A June 1980 decree described the contracts required for the transfer of state properties to municipalities. It also outlined the regular audits of municipal finances and subventions that the Contraloría General de la República, the government agency responsible for audits and issues of constitutionality, would perform. The decree stipulated that personnel working in transferred services would have the option of either surrendering their status as civil servants, transferring their pension benefits to a private pension manager (AFP), and receiving severance pay, or remaining under the government salary and pension benefit systems without receiving severance pay (Decreto con Fuerza de Ley No. 1-3063, June 2, 1980). The severance pay was set high enough to win over the support of teachers in the transferred schools, enticing almost all of them to enter the private sector in 1981.

A decree law of August 1980 established a uniform subvention for private and municipal schools. The subvention's value was to be tied to an indexed unit of account, the *unidad tributaria mensual* (UTM), and would vary according to the costs associated with the level of education being taught and the geographic location of the school. This decree authorized the Corporation for the Construction of Educational Establishments, the legal entity that possessed the title to the school buildings, to enter into leasing contracts with the municipalities for periods of ninety-nine years.[10]

A September 1980 decree law authorized extraordinary payments to municipalities to cover the costs associated with the transfer of schools and health clinics. These payments were to be 5 percent of the annual expenditures associated with the transferred service in 1980, 4 percent of the same in 1981, and 3 percent in 1982. The same decree also included an interesting modification to Article 38 of the Law of Municipal Revenues that permitted municipalities to delegate the management of schools and clinics to subsidiary private corporations. The amendment held that municipal governments, "for the purposes of the administration and operation of [transferred services], will be able to form, in accord with the norms of Title XXXIII of Book I of the Civil Code, together with organizations of the community interested in the said services, one or more not-for-profit, juridical persons of private standing" (Decreto Ley 3477, September 2, 1980).

The government transferred 362 schools and their 3,097 teachers to municipalities on December 31, 1980. For symbolic reasons, the regime wanted the beginnings of the new educational system to coincide with the new constitution, which was to take effect on March 11, 1981. The reluctance of officials in the Ministry of Finance to pay teachers according to the scale established in the 1978 Teachers' Law (Ley de Carrera Docente), an increasingly expensive piece of legislation, was a second cause for the haste in which the educational system was constructed.[11]

By April 1982, when the regime suspended the transfer process because the economic crash had depleted the treasury of the funds required for teacher severance pay, some 84–87 percent of all state schools in the country had been turned over to municipalities.[12] Meanwhile the percentage of students attending private subsidized schools, which the new subvention structure was designed to increase, rose from 15 percent to 22 percent between 1980 and 1983, while enrollment share fell from 78 percent to 71 percent in the state and municipal schools over the same period. In 1987 the military government transferred those schools that remained under the jurisdiction of the Ministry of Education to municipalities. With those transfers the governance of the Chilean primary and secondary educational system assumed its present form.

The democratic government did not change the essential structure of the educational system that it inherited from the Pinochet regime. Chapter 4 explores the reasons for this in more detail, but here a few comments will suffice. Despite the views of leaders in the teachers' union[13] and some in the Radical and Socialist Parties, who advocated the return of the management and ownership of schools to the Ministry of Education, the Concertación remained committed to the municipal control of schools and to the subvention mechanism. This was partly policy choice: after the long period of soul-searching and exile that followed the coup, the center and left intellectual Socialists and Christian Democrats had "renovated" their social and economic philosophies (Puryear 1994). It is certainly true, however, that several problems—sizeable debt service and a floor for defense spending, concern for macroeconomic stability, and the need for political accommodation under the terms of the 1980 Constitution—forced the recalcitrant groups in the Concertación government to accept large elements of the post-welfare model.

The Chilean educational system as it stands, then, retains most of the key elements of the neoliberal design. Senior officials in the Ministry of Education under the Aylwin and Frei governments have believed that the state ought to play a more active role in promoting the educational needs of the poor and supporting local autonomy than the military government allowed it. But they have concurred with the neoliberal notion of strengthening municipal control at the expense of the ministry, whose new role is to set national norms, measure local achievement, and intervene only when necessary. A senior education advisor under Aylwin and Frei characterized the new role for the state in these terms:

> So the new role of the state is manifest in the education sectors and can be characterized in metaphoric language: "from planning and policy making as engineering to planning and policy making as gardening." In other words, a passage from a system where the

key decisions emanate from a center to a system where the localities conceive of themselves as self-governing organizational authorities, which obtain from the center the information and the means
necessary for independent growth but function on their own initiative, are responsible for their own management, and are capable
of adapting to their environment. (Cox 1993, 126)

The Center Holds

Despite the fact that municipalities and private school owners now own
and manage schools in the Chilean subsidized sector, few people doubt that
the "key decisions emanate from the center." Despite the "modernization" of
the sector, individuals, whether as voters or consumers, are not in control of
educational decisions. Three kinds of barriers have prevented them from
exercising power: the central government continues to wield substantial and
discretionary power in the sector, municipalities have replicated a hierarchical organization at the local level, and tensions between "exit" and "voice"
options in the system limit the effectiveness of political and economic signals.

The role of the Ministry of Education is supposedly limited to "technical-pedagogical" issues, with administration left to municipalities and private
school owners; but the "technical" role permits it wide-ranging discretionary
power. To grant a degree, a school must first be recognized as a "collaborator
in the educational function of the state," which means it must adhere to the
ministry's curricula or propose its own, which few schools have the capacity
to do, and it must possess adequate teaching materials, a "qualified" staff, and
a suitable building.[14] To qualify for subventions, a school must also set its
class sizes within the ministry's limits, possess a complete cycle of elementary
and/or secondary education, charge its students no more than the small fees
deemed permissible, and pay the salaries and social security of its employees.
Failure to comply with these and other rules can result in penalties ranging
from a fine to a permanent cancellation of state recognition. Approval from
the ministerial regional secretariat (SEREMI) is also required for the sale or
transfer of a school, a change of address, a merger between schools, and for
the creation of a new level or type of education within an existing school.[15]

In 1986, in response to mounting protests over the alleged abuses of private subsidized schools from newly emboldened actors in civil society,[16] the
ministry imposed an exacting series of requirements for infrastructure in private subsidized schools. The decrees were very detailed, listing, for example,

measurements for minimum classroom floor space as a function of school size, chair dimensions for students of varying heights, and surface areas for laboratory tables. The precision of the measurements, combined with the discretion given to the SEREMIs in determining the manner and timing of enforcement, made the regulations extremely costly and difficult to comply with and led hundreds of private subsidized schools to close down.[17] Although the 1986 restrictions are no longer in force, the ministry retains the power to enforce requirements strictly or leniently, depending on, among other things, its political interests. Even if it rarely shuts a school down altogether, the threat to do so forces municipal and private schools to consult with it on most serious decisions.

The ministry enforces its rules by means of an inspection system. Auditors from the ministerial provincial directorates (DIRPROVs) randomly check the schools under their jurisdiction, with a particular interest in the school's physical state, possession of necessary documents, conformity with ministerial norms, and actual and recent attendance records. The last is especially important to the ministry because falsifications of attendance cheat the state out of subvention payments. Although the ministry's focus is supposedly pedagogical and not administrative, violations in record keeping receive larger fines than pedagogical violations, such as granting a degree to a student who is not qualified to graduate (Circular 606, Ministry of Education, undated). Because the inspectors are usually officials trained under the old educational system, which emphasized hierarchies and standardization, municipal education directors and private school owners spend a great deal of time avoiding penalties.

The scope of the inspections has steadily expanded over the years, especially for private schools. Realizing in 1983 that no mechanism existed to enforce the minimal educational requirements for receiving a subvention, the ministry authorized the SEREMIs to inspect schools for safety and hygiene and gave the provincial directorates authority to establish required teaching materials for each school (Decreto Supremo 81/83, August 1, 1983; Decreto Supremo 615/83, August 13, 1983). When the economy crashed in 1983, the ministry suspected that private subsidized schools were hiding small payments received from parents to avoid having to remit a fraction of those receipts to the national treasury. It therefore required elaborate lists of all payments and donations received.[18] Other laws require schools to keep documents on hand that verify conformity with physical, health, and safety standards of the Ministries of Education, Health, and Housing. Private school buildings are also subject to inspection by the public works departments of the municipalities, with whom the schools compete for student enrollments. All told, the government monitors private schools more closely and frequently than at any other time in Chilean history, a surpassingly paradoxical outcome for a neoliberal project (Magendzo et al. 1988).

The inspections and central government rules raise the costs of innovation for both municipal and private schools. Few are experimenting. All schools must adhere to given curricula, organize themselves in normal cycles, and operate in a traditional building. A 1991 law requires all teachers to have completed degrees in pedagogy except for those working on temporary contracts, who cannot constitute more than 20 percent of the teaching staff of any school (Ley No. 19.070, July 1, 1991, "Estatuto Docente"). Because the state sets the norms for teachers' education in public and private universities and professional institutes, teachers in all schools share similar backgrounds and pedagogical orientations. Ministerial decrees, in the exacting spirit of Chilean legalism, regulate administration in schools, elaborating subcategories and specifying the functions and purposes of the director, subdirector, general inspector, technical-pedagogical unit, administrative unit, coordinating council, teachers' council, unit of production, parents' association, and student organization.[19] After the reform process was well underway, the ministry continued to act as if it were running schools: it enumerated the documents municipal schools were permitted to keep on hand (forbidding all others), set grading scales for all schools and determined the number and types of tests to be administered each semester in each year of study, categorized teaching personnel in ranks (including "projectionists" and "special teaching guides"), required SEREMI approval for the selection of municipal school names (public and private subsidized), and specified nationwide colors for public and private school student uniforms. (The ministry later did allow principals to select a color for their school tie.)[20] The neoliberal reforms promoting private education have not led to educational diversity, innovation, and experimentation in Chile but have in fact brought more state controls to private education, arguably even increasing homogeneity in an already uniform system.[21]

Chilean policy makers, society, and even the courts continue to believe that it is the ministry that is effectively running the municipal schools. Municipal schools did not, for example, have to apply for recognition as "collaborators in the educational function of the state" but were granted that status automatically (Decreto 8143, September 25, 1990). A ruling of the Tribunal Constitucional held that the municipalities could not delegate their educational responsibilities to autonomous, private corporations because this would mean that the state was relinquishing its constitutionally mandated educational responsibility.[22] Although the Ministry of Education permits municipal and private schools to award certificates at the completion of elementary school, it reserved the authority to grant all high school diplomas in the nation. The title of secondary school teachers remains "Profesor de Estado."

Although a specific historical legacy and set of political relationships promote the Chilean central government's continuing intervention in decentralized and privatized schools (these are described in chapter 4), that intervention also illustrates a general problem in the post-welfare model for education. Education is constitutive of citizenship, which by its nature must be understood and debated at the most general level, in national laws established by the most representative bodies. The tendency of central governments to regulate educative enterprises has its source, then, in this very old idea that citizenship entails a kind of uniformity and generality. While states might seek "collaborators" in their educational function, all of them implicitly or explicitly guarantee its generality. Traditionally, they did so by managing schools themselves; but more recently and under the influence of post-welfare theorists, they do so by laying down the "rules of the game" and letting other entities provide educational services, in the manner that states do not run restaurants but do guarantee food safety. But the Chilean experience suggests that it is very difficult for states to extricate themselves from the educative enterprise, that the transfer of state finances and authority to private agents leads to a gradual expansion of state supervision and oversight as the problem of guaranteeing the generality of citizenship grows more complex. The perceived need for that guarantee is felt all the more strongly in education because the service recipients, children, are vulnerable. The problem for post-welfare theory, then, is that guaranteeing generality is much more difficult than guaranteeing safety. No consensus exists on the meaning of citizenship in general: like knowledge itself, it is always contested and always changing. While this problem is acute for education, it is also true for other social sectors such as health care, in which access to and the prioritization of services constitute social citizenship in the modern world, and which as a result calls for fairness at the most general level.

A second obstacle to effective decentralization, and to the gains post-welfare theorists believe would follow from localizing decision making power, is that information is often no better in municipalities than it is at the national level. At the time of the municipal transfers in Chile, many alcaldes were captains and colonels appointed directly by Pinochet. They had little or no experience in education or management, and neither they nor their staffs were equipped to assess local employment needs and adjust their educational programs to them, as the theoreticians of neoliberal reform had hoped.[23] The alcaldes were military men accustomed to following precise orders, which they received from their military and administrative superiors throughout the period. Most notably, they were told whom not to fire and how to use extraordinary payments.[24] The municipalization project suffered from a fundamental contradiction: although for the neoliberal planners in the government decentralization was designed to increase local powers, for the military it was the lowest rung of the national command and control structure.

In 1992, more than ten years after the education reforms, Chilean alcaldes were popularly elected for the first time. Although electoral independence would seem to promise more autonomous and more locally sensitive decision making, that has not happened. No municipality, for instance, had delineated a community-specific plan for education in 1994, with the noteworthy exception of Las Condes, a wealthy *comuna* in eastern Santiago, which was implementing a system of merit pay for its teachers, establishing a "university track" in one of its high schools, and ceding more authority to school directors. The Ley Orgánica Constitucional de Enseñanza establishes and guards a space for local initiative in educational policy making, but almost no municipalities possess the technical level, foresight, and courage to develop their own educational policies.

The shortcomings in local capacity, widely cited as a key problem during the decentralization process, are legion in Chile. The number of employees in government who are professionals has not increased noticeably as a result of the reforms (Marcel 1993, 30). The salaries of municipal employees fell substantially during the 1980s, making it less attractive than the private sector to potential officials. Changes in the permanent staff of each municipality must be ratified by law or approved by the president. Municipal employees enjoy the protection of the Estatuto Adminstrativo, or civil service protection, and are difficult to dismiss. Because of the low salaries, the legacy of arbitrary dismissals at the beginning of the military government, the virtual freeze in promotions and advancements in municipal government that followed the dismissals, and the limited powers granted municipal workers, municipal civil service is considered second-rate government work in most parts of the country.

A further reason for local inertia is that municipal governments enjoy far less financial autonomy than public choice theory would prescribe. The central government sets uniform national tax rates, including the rates on commercial patents, automobile licenses, and property, which together constitute the main sources of municipal revenue. The central government has also granted exemptions on property taxes and commercial patents on the basis of political influence for decades: over half the properties in the country are tax-exempt (Marcel 1993). All municipal expenditures and revenues, including the educational subventions and the diagnosis-related payments to municipal primary health clinics, are subject to monthly audits by the Contraloría General de la República. Given the technical capacity of most municipalities, oversight is necessary; but its frequency consumes the time and limits the autonomy of municipal officials. The Constitution of 1980 prevents municipalities from issuing debt, which only increases the municipal demand for government transfers, promoting a further expansion of central powers and taxation. Compounding the irrationalities, municipalities often circumvent the indebtedness constraint and effectively borrow by leasing equipment and by occasionally delaying the social security payments for employees. These various constraints on municipal financial powers make impossible the fit between local preferences and tax rates that public choice theory deems optimal. Although municipalities can set commercial license rates within a narrow band, the power to tax remains a prerogative of the central government.[25]

The educational departments within municipalities are as a rule very weak. The Constitutional Organic Law of Municipalities, which establishes the organizational structure for all municipalities in the country, does not mention the municipal department of education (DEM), which leaves it without any constitutional standing in the municipality and therefore dependent on another unit, often the division of community development. The division of administration and finance receives the educational subventions from the Ministry of Finance in most municipalities. The DEM, then, generally manages no resources, makes no expenditure decisions, and remains outside the flow of important information within the municipality. The head of the department is by law a civil service teacher and not a political confidante appointed by the alcalde, compounding the political weakness of the DEM. The stated functions of the DEMs are hiring teachers to fill vacancies, complying with DIRPROV requests for information and inspections, and proposing the size of municipal teaching endowments; but often the DEM finds itself a "mail box" for the passing of papers.[26]

Although the Chilean municipal tradition is particularly weak, even by Latin American standards, and although Chile's local governments will almost certainly grow both stronger and more participatory, these problems

do illustrate a second general problem in the post-welfare conception of educational services. Theoretically, information about local needs is better the
"closer" the government and the more disaggregated the political and economic signals that providers receive. The theory does not recognize, however
that information is not merely a function of the signals themselves but of the
actions of the individuals involved: if policy makers want good information
about needs in the social sectors, they must participate in their articulation
Individuals will not express their preferences to local officials if the officials
are not ready to hear and elicit them, which will not occur when local capacity is weak, when municipal powers are perceived to be ineffective, and when
those officials who can best diagnose and hear educational preferences have
a low status. Decentralization, though it shields officials from organized
interest group influences at the national level, will not necessarily lead
providers to listen to the needs of constituents instead. Needs in education
and other social sector services are not obvious and self-evident: they take
shape and meaning only through the interaction of governments and individuals.

Obstacles to local control of education include not only hierarchical

*Children study together in a school near Temuco, 1996. Courtesy of the Economic
Development Institute of the World Bank.*

organization at the central and the local levels but contradictions within the system. First, political and economic signals can conflict. Because in the "choice" model educational services are not linked to a region of residence, most Chilean municipal schools educate students whose families do not live in that municipality. (Attending any public school is an option that has existed for a long time in Chile, but the educational modernization gave it new emphasis.) The more the number of out-of-region students attending a given municipality's schools, the less the electoral pressure on its alcalde to improve the quality of the schools under his management. In the wealthy *comunas* of Providencia and Santiago, for example, which have long been known for running some of the best public schools in the nation, some 73 percent and 80 percent, respectively, of the students come from outside the municipalities (*El Mercurio,* September 18, 1993). Political and economic signals function at cross-purposes in the Chilean system: a rise in school quality increases demand for admission, resulting in a more able student population but also one composed of a greater percentage of out-of-region students, which in turn reduces the political pressure on the alcalde to improve the municipality's schools.

A second problem in the global coherence of signals is that the exit of elites from the public system continues unabated. Because most Chilean political, cultural, and economic elites send their children to private paid schools outside of the subsidized "choice" system, political support for the subventions is relatively weak. Having grown accustomed to the exit option from state schools, Chilean elites discount the urgency of voicing complaints about the subsidized schools because their children are not affected. Hirschman makes this point:

> Suppose at some point, for whatever reason, the public schools deteriorate. Thereupon, increasing numbers of quality-education-conscious parents will send their children to private schools. This "exit" may occasion some impulse toward an improvement of the public schools; but here again this impulse is far less significant than the loss to the public schools of those member-customers who would be most motivated and determined to put up a fight against the deterioration if they did not have the alternative of the private schools. (Hirschman 1970, 45–46)

Finally, the partitioning of information between various local and central government agencies limits effective decision making and obscures accountability. For example, while one set of organs, the DIRPROVs and the DEMs, establishes the teaching endowment size for schools and proposes transfers, another evaluates teaching quality. Although information on teaching quality would influence decisions on endowment size, the DEMs do not receive it. The municipalities were legal arms of the Ministry of the Interior until 1989 (and in some cases remain technically and normatively dependent on it) while the Ministry of Education supervised municipal schools. This "dual dependency" created rivalries and unclear responsibilities. The division of authority between local and central agents, as well as among ministries, also allows all branches of government to avoid some of the political pressure to improve school quality by shifting the burden of accountability.

Teachers' Incentives and Teachers' Power

Post-welfare advocates believe that public sector service delivery promotes mediocrity because providers have no incentive to satisfy their clients. A system utilizing market forces, on the other hand, rewards providers who perform well. In educational choice, the idea, in simplest terms, is that school owners or managers will dismiss slack teachers while rewarding the talented ones with higher salaries because their own profits or salaries depend on attracting more students. The Chilean military regime attempted to create a post-welfare incentive structure in both the private subsidized and municipal sectors by revoking teachers' civil service tenure, effectively abolishing the pay scale, outlawing collective bargaining, and linking school finance to attendance rates. The market forces could not operate effectively, however, because decision making in the authoritarian regime remained highly centralized, local officials could not easily replace ineffective teachers, the links between revenues and teachers' reputations were found to be tenuous and sluggish, the effects on morale of declining real wages and diminished status outweighed monetary incentives, and the organization of the teaching profession continued to constrain its potential dynamism.

The idea of firing ineffective teachers opposed a decades-long tradition of stable employment in education that could not be transformed overnight. Those responsible for managing schools and implementing the new competitive atmosphere, the alcaldes, were themselves educated in the *estado docente* and could not internalize the new tasks that the modernized system asked of them. They were also military officials, for whom hierarchy and control, not instability and change, is the guiding principle. Although they did fire teachers for budgetary reasons and for allegedly leftist ties, they almost never dismissed poorly performing teachers when they had the opportunity to do so because they did not see that as their task. One alcalde's boast in 1985 is representative of the unreconstructed paternalism, linked to the tradition of stable employment in education, that they exhibited: "When the transfer was made, I thought they were going to give me one teacher for every forty or forty-five students, but it turned out that they transferred me a surplus of teachers. I have not fired a single one. We've arranged the schedules so that my teachers—the teachers of our children and our grandchildren—are relaxed, and we've even tried to increase their salaries."[27]

The military regime never even gave the alcaldes the political freedom to dismiss teachers on their own: almost universally, alcaldes would wait for orders to come down before acting. During the economic crisis of 1982–83, in the face of rising unemployment and mounting political protest, the regime ordered the alcaldes not to lay off any teachers. When the economy had recovered and municipal deficits were emerging as a problem in 1986, the municipalities were then told to dismiss some eight thousand teachers. Those decisions were made at the highest level, in secret, and with little or no input from the alcaldes.[28] Similarly, the private subsidized schools were on the whole more concerned with keeping salary costs down than with improving school quality. On finding that client response in the short term would not change much if they hired exceptional teachers, they tended to hire young teachers at low salaries. In general, Chilean school teachers did grow to fear being laid off under the new system, but their probability of dismissal appeared unrelated to their performance.

Despite their specifically authoritarian context, the Chilean reforms illustrate a pair of broader problems in the microeconomic argument linking labor market liberalization to better incentives in education. First, teachers are not mobile and easily replaceable factors of production. As long as the government restricts the labor supply, limiting the number of teaching degrees awarded partly in response to political pressures, threats to dismiss large numbers of poorly performing teachers and hire new ones are not credible. Nor is the threat to lure away teachers from other schools as a matter of practice. Because in most countries teachers are women with families and because compensation is low relative to moving costs, moving from one school to another, even for a better salary, often does not pay. In addition, changing teachers in the middle of an academic year, or dismissing a number of them all at once, can be detrimental to learning even if the new teachers are better than the old ones. One thing teachers provide is a stable, safe environment for learning, a good that is sensitive to disturbances; and a school might choose, therefore, to tolerate a mediocre teacher for educational reasons. Schools in rural or urban marginal areas experience particular difficulty attracting enough teachers. All of these considerations work to minimize the credibility of firing threats and their alleged benefits for teaching quality and productivity: one reason that the Chilean private school owners and alcaldes did not attempt to improve school quality with the threat of dismissals is that the educational process requires stable relationships.

A second general problem is that the tie between teacher performance and salaries is tenuous and sluggish. A good teacher will bring in additional revenues only if more students choose the school on the basis of her teaching. Given the highly imperfect information parents possess about school quality in countries like Chile, good teaching might have no effect on school profits; and even if it does, there will be a delay of one or more years because reputations take time to form. And when new clients do choose a school, it will be difficult to determine which teacher, if any, deserves credit for the school's increase in market share. Unlike lawyers in a partnership, whose value is measured by the clients they bring in, teacher salaries will have a more tenuous link to their firms' revenues. There is also the possibility that imperfect information will lead to perverse incentives. If a school tries to reward teachers who are performing well, utilizing improvements in class test scores to measure success, teachers will vie with one other for the most teachable students, which will lead to wasted energies and internecine competition. Merit pay, then, might work only for teams of teachers or for schools as a whole (Murmane and Cohen 1986). Problems such as these contributed to the failure of a 1981 proposal that would have linked teacher salaries to test score performance in Chile, and they complicate the fit between compensation and performance that the post-welfare structures aim to create.

The overall working conditions of teachers deteriorated drastically during the reform decade, overwhelming whatever effects the new incentive structure might have had. In the municipal and private subsidized sectors combined, about one-fifth of the 100,000 teachers in Chile lost their jobs at least once between 1980 and 1989, and teachers saw their real wages decline over 30 percent on average between those same years. Large numbers of teachers were forced to work two shifts a day or take on part-time jobs. They also saw their professional status and their standing in society decline markedly (Gysling 1992; Lomnitz and Melnick 1991; Calvo 1984). The 1981 reform in higher education, for example, did not count teaching among the professions requiring university training, and over twenty "professional institutes" began to offer two-year degrees in pedagogy. Teachers found themselves subject to decision making on the part of alcaldes and school owners with no pedagogical training or expertise, which they found insulting. The military regime's program to disarticulate rival political organizations targeted the teachers' union in particular because of its undeserved reputation as an instrument of the Communist and Socialist Parties.

The demoralization of teachers associated with the new educational system in Chile is not uncommon in post-welfare reform efforts. Because the ideology of these reforms usually deprecates governments and bureaucracies while lauding privatization, the nobility of public service, which for long has been one of the career's primary rewards, grows obsolete. Civil servants dedicate themselves to their work with less passion when the value of that dedication is questioned. If the post-welfare organization could abolish bureaucracies outright, the problem might be merely to understand the nostalgia for the lost ideal of public service. In reality, however, post-welfare reforms require governmental bodies to perform new and often more complicated tasks—measuring service quality, arbitrating disputes, encouraging local initiative and participation—while eviscerating their social and ideological foundations. If the post-welfare reforms include a transitional period, which they almost always do, or involve decentralization rather than privatization, the neoliberal assault on government becomes self-fulfilling. O'Donnell describes the problem:

> Specialized bureaucracies have been decapitated by the exodus of their most qualified employees, management is increasingly politicized, repeated "rationalizations" and "reorganizations" have failed, and physical plant decay has advanced dramatically. . . . These conditions provide fertile soil for a poorly motivated and unskilled bureaucracy, which, in turn, feeds the innumerable anecdotes that fuel the all-out assault on the state. Meanwhile, the political support needed for effecting a more balanced government policy toward its own apparatus is eroded. (O'Donnell 1994)

Finally, one variant of post-welfare thinking particularly influential in diagnoses of the incentive structures of educational systems, in which teachers are not necessarily lazy or rent-seeking but merely victims of bureaucratic control, simplifies both the causes of and the solutions to the origins of the relative weakness of teachers in educational systems. Centralism has deep roots in the Chilean educative process that financing changes alone cannot easily transform. Every school possesses a "technical-pedagogical unit" that determines the frequency and number of grades administered in each class, and each subject area has a "head teacher" and subordinates. Inspectors who report directly to the principal monitor the halls, watching not only the haircuts and dress of students but the promptness and appearance of teachers. Until relatively recently principals were required to evaluate their teachers on the same 1 to 7 scale used for student grades, casting the same infantilizing gaze on teachers that the teachers fixed on students. Although teachers are no longer state employees, their behaviors remain subject to the kind of close scrutiny ideal foremen apply to assembly workers, belying the industrial and enlightenment origins of the Chilean (and most other) educational systems. Obviously, that is an impediment to the dynamism and creativity that post-welfare advocates seek.

The Chubb and Moe (1992) theory of educational choice attempts to explain the reasons for the absence of dynamism and creativity in education and the roots of the sector's poor incentive structure. The writers argue that bureaucratic rules rigidify in order to consolidate the gains of political winners. When allies of the educational unions win elections, they seek to maintain privileges for their supporters with rules that codify them: tenure laws, limits on curricular innovations, regulations guaranteeing gainful employment for counselors and other education workers. As a result, the professional discretion of teachers and the autonomy of individual schools inevitably decline. Their theory fits the sequence of events in Chile during the reemergence of democratic politics reasonably well. In 1991 the government reintroduced teacher tenure and established explicit rules constraining hiring and firing procedures in order to eliminate arbitrary dismissals. It also reestablished a national experience-based pay scale and codified the rights of the teaching profession in school decision making. In some sense the law signified a return to the tradition of Chile's so-called *estado de compromiso,* the implicit pact among Chilean political parties to respect each other's patronage appointments so that each party could guarantee its clients and constituents the future benefits of current spoils. While their account of interest group politics in education is useful, Chubb and Moe's solution to the problem, however—a privatization that eliminates the arena in which interest groups act—overestimates the importance of interest group politics in education and underestimates the relevant characteristics of teaching itself.

The source of the relative weakness of educators is not only bureaucratic control, rigidities that consolidate political gains, but the limited nature of "technical autonomy" in the field of education (Friedson 1986). Because every educated person can claim a degree of expertise in the area, pedagogical knowledge cannot attain the respect and power accorded to the stronger professions such as medicine and law. If it were only a case of political "capture" by teachers' unions, the same outcome would be expected in law, medicine, and the other professions. Political capture presupposes that the provider groups need to capture state agencies, which teachers would not, if like doctors in the United States, they were strong enough to secure their interests privately. Because technical autonomy in elementary and secondary school teaching is not well established, educators are open to control from other powers, such as state governments in the United States or political parties in Chile. Breaking up the state monopoly on education, then, though it might liberate schools from one form of bureaucratic control, would not necessarily lead to effective schools because educators on the whole would remain weak, and open to control from new sources, such as municipal governments, school owners, or the uninformed public.

"Effective schools," autonomous institutions that emphasize clear academic goals in a coherent environment, rarely appear in the public sector not only because small schools are more expensive and bureaucratic rules limit professional discretion, but because larger schools more easily accommodate the diversity of beliefs concerning educational ends that prevail in liberal polities. Bigger schools, for example, can field sports teams and other extracurricular programs, whose socializing value for many families exceeds the potential loss in academic achievement resulting from larger size. While choice theory argues that educators or educational bureaucrats wrest schools away from the families that schools are intended to serve, it misses a prior event: society or other agents capture educational systems at the expense of the educators' professional interest in making schools serve an educative end that they alone can provide.

This is becoming evident to Chilean education policy makers who, recognizing the need to empower teachers, now call "pedagogical decentralization" the task of the 1990s. The government's MECE program, for instance, encourages and funds a limited number of curricular initiatives from teachers or other groups. In another effort, the ministry permits schools to replace the official curricula with ones of their own design, although very few subsidized schools have successfully created their own educational plans.[29] These programs constitute an understanding that the professional status of teachers is at least as important as the institutional design of the educational system in Chile. Whether the professional status of teachers can be changed without also addressing the problem of technical autonomy, however, is a serious question.

Educational Financing and School Choice

Financial shortages, inconsistencies, and disparities have plagued the Chilean educational system. Some of the financial problems were avoidable or contingent, but others, particularly an inherent tension between central-ized funding and municipal autonomy, appear intrinsic to the post-welfare model in small developing countries. Examining the underfinancing of the Chilean reforms and its effects following the economic crisis of 1981 makes this clear.

Faced with unemployment that would reach 30 percent, a current account crisis, the collapse of the banking system, and an inevitable peso devaluation bringing ignominy upon its economic team, the regime sus-pended the monthly indexation of educational subventions and cut subven-tion values by 5 percent in 1981. Their value would be tied to occasional increases in public sector wages, and as a result would decline 32 percent in real terms between December 1980 and November 1991.[30] Subsidized schools were chronically underfunded during the period, leading to real reductions in teacher salaries, infrastructure investments, teaching material acquisitions, and teacher training. Most subsidized schools operated (and continue to operate) two shifts per day, effectively running two separate schools in the same establishment, leaving youth with nothing to do for half the day, an arrangement that some observers associate with the rise in delin-quency and drug addiction over the period. (President Frei's recent education initiative would invest US$1.5 billion to lengthen the school day to one shift of eight pedagogical hours.) In that economic climate, autonomous decision making on the part of the private subsidized schools and localities was impossible. None of the schools had the resources to experiment with new approaches, compete for the best teachers, or institute performance-based incentives for its employees. Some schools operated without a box for petty cash: payments for even routine activities, like purchasing additional chalk or making extra copies of an assignment, required approval from department heads. In one informal survey, more than 90 percent of municipal education departments, driven to austerity, were setting strict school budgets with no input from their principals (Lavin 1993, 45). Under conditions of extreme underfinancing, the possibility of school autonomy disappears.

The democratic government in 1990 passed a tax increase for the pur-pose of repaying the "social debt" accumulated during the 1980s, primarily in education and health. Real education spending increased over 30 percent in the first four years of democratic rule, and the real value of the subventions finally recovered all of the ground it had lost following the deindexation of 1982. The Estatuto Docente, mentioned above, set a gradually rising floor for all teacher salaries in the country. It established an experience-based pay scale for the municipal sector; and, using revenues from the 1990 tax legislation, the central government created a special fund to help municipalities meet the mandated salary levels for the teachers in their schools. The Estatuto Docente also created funds for schools in marginal or rural areas and for continuing professional education.

These new revenue sources, as well as the experience-based pay scale, constitute a substantial departure from the post-welfare model because they transfer resources not as a subsidy to demand but to providers on the basis of input costs. Moreover, by sending some resources to municipalities but not to private subsidized schools, the Estatuto slants the playing field, which the neoliberals had tried to make as level as possible in the belief that public-private competition would improve education.

In reality, however, Chile had deviated from the theory almost from the beginning. The deindexation of the subventions resulted in a problem and a decision that still plagues the Chilean system: municipal deficits, which the government chose to allay with extraordinary transfers outside of the subventions. Alcaldes had been going to the office of the superintendent for help with special projects in the early 1980s, and a few especially noteworthy proposals had received the support of Superintendent Maria Teresa Infante, who solicited and received extraordinary outlays from the Ministry of Finance. When the subvention level started to decline sharply in real terms and as the municipal sector began to lose substantial numbers of students to private subsidized schools, more and more alcaldes began to request assistance to cover basic costs. On a regular basis, various government officials from the Ministries of Education, Finance, and the Interior, and the regional governors, *intendentes,* and alcaldes met, bargained, negotiated, pleaded, and lobbied for additional outlays to cover the costs of municipal education. These extra payments were not allocated on the basis of any public formula, and their values probably owed as much to military politics as to objective assessments of need. Deficit coverage became quasi-institutionalized. In 1986, and again in 1989, the government studied the problem and proposed measures to phase out the deficits, such as an increase in subvention values, firing excess teachers, and rationalizing municipal services; but officials did not implement any of these proposals comprehensively enough to eliminate the deficit problem (Ministerio de Educación 1986, Ministerio de Hacienda 1989). By 1985, 201 municipalities (out of 325) were experiencing a combined annual deficit of over 2.1 billion pesos, or roughly 7 percent of the total value of subvention transfers to municipalities in that year. The corresponding figures for 1986 and 1987 were 3.1 billion pesos, or 8 percent, and 4.3 billion pesos, or 8.5 percent, respectively.[31]

The democratic regime inherited municipal deficits, but it treats them differently. First, deficit coverage is based on the formula for the fund that redistributes municipal revenues, the fondo común municipal (FCM), a measure that seeks to remove these side payments from the arena of political bargaining. Second, according to the government, the deficits should be understood not as the difference between municipal subvention revenues and education costs, but that difference once municipal educational management has been rationalized. The ministry believes that subventions now suffice to cover school operating costs in most cases and that shortfalls are generally the result of excessive, politically motivated employment. Although few good studies of municipal education departments and corporations exist, some evidence collected in the subsecretariat for regional development (SUBDERE) suggests that a number of municipalities are running "deficits" because they employ too many administrators. An investigation found that the educational corporations of several municipalities had in fact hired several times the number recorded on their official books.[32]

The Association of Municipalities, however, claims that the central government underestimates the costs of managing schools, that the subvention level is too low, and that additional transfers to cover deficits remain necessary. The revenues that some municipalities contribute to education are taken from other municipal services, such as community lighting, road maintenance, improving education facilities, and sanitation, or are even withdrawn illegally from the pension payments for municipal employees. The association estimates that the total municipal contribution, its "deficit," was 32 thousand million pesos in 1993, constituting about 7 percent of total municipal revenues and about 26 percent of subvention revenues. The average municipality spent 14 percent of its own revenues on educational services in 1993 (Ministerio de Educación 1994).

The Estatuto Docente makes it unlawful for municipalities to dismiss teachers on the grounds of a decline in enrollment, or even to transfer a teacher to another school with greater enrollment without her consent. As a result, irrationalities in the distribution of teachers and failures to take advantage of economies of scale mar the municipal sector. While the average class size in private subsidized schools pushes the allowable limit of 45, the student-teacher ratio in the municipal sector is 21 to 1.[33] The central government claims that the subvention is not predicated on classes of that small a size, and it cites empirical studies that fail to find a connection between class size and educational outcomes. The government has tried repeatedly to restore municipal authority to dismiss or transfer teachers for reasons of a drop in enrollment, but the teachers' union has gone on strike several times to fight the proposal. A related issue is teacher hiring. While municipal student enrollment grew 2.9 percent from 1991 to 1994, the total number of teachers in the sector grew by 9.6 percent, and the number of teacher hours contracted grew 5.9 percent.[34] The Estatuto Docente established a supposedly neutral mechanism for setting the teacher endowment level of each municipality: the municipal department of education (DEM) proposes a number, the ministerial provincial directorate (DIRPROV) reviews and perhaps contests it, and a joint meeting of the subsecretariat for regional development (SUBDERE), the Ministry of Education, and the municipality (usually represented not by the DEM head but by the alcaldes), settles disagreements. Given the recent increase in teachers hired during a period of declining enrollment, this procedure has apparently failed to eliminate politics from school staffing.[35]

The deficits and the government's decision to help offset them in the 1980s subverted the post-welfare design. It turned subvention financing, which was supposed to impose competitive discipline on the subsidized sector, into a soft budget constraint. It forced the central government to intervene heavily in the municipalized system. In 1985, in an effort to save money, the ministry directed the SEREMIs to consider "whether the educational needs of the region and locality justify the existence of new establishments" before authorizing the founding of new private subsidized schools. Subsecretary René Salamé, responsible for the new provision, argued that since these schools were using state funds, the state had an obligation to see that the money was not wasted on unnecessary or redundant services.[36] He expressed the state's role in unequivocal terms: "the hand of the government will not hesitate to sanction those private schools that make improper use of the subventions authorized by the state for the financing of operations" (Magendzo et al. 1988, 136).

In the democratic regime, the central government continues to involve itself in issues of school management, such as the size of municipal education staffs, because political hirings at the local level cost the national treasury. They also affect national fiscal policy and worry the Ministry of Finance and the central bank, which are intent on keeping inflation in the single digits. This problem illustrates a general tension in the post-welfare model, particularly for small developing countries: because the central government wants to maintain control of the budget and fiscal policy, it is forced to involve itself in setting the staff endowments for local school districts.

The same logic can operate in reverse: when unemployment rates are high, the central government is tempted to intervene in educational administration to prevent further job loss or slow declines in real wages. A 1984 law required subsidized private schools, who had been dismissing teachers in late December and rehiring them in late February, to pay summer wages for teachers.[37] Other decrees required private subsidized schools to use fixed percentages of subventions received in certain months for teachers' bonus pay.[38] In a small country with nationalized educational funding but local administrative control, the national macroeconomic targets, whether inflation or employment, will impinge on local and private sector education staffing decisions.

The new educational system in Chile also results in disparities. Because municipalities can contribute their own funds to school operations, a revenue source unconnected to exit signals is available unequally between municipal and private subsidized sectors and unequally among the municipalities. Tax receipts (primarily through real estate taxes), commercial permit requests, and the demand for automobile licenses, the main sources of municipal revenue, vary widely among the municipalities. Some of the wealthier *comunas* double the subvention through their own contributions to municipal education while others manage contributions of less than 20 percent of the subvention's annualized value. Chile's municipal tax system includes a redistributive mechanism, the *fondo común municipal* (FCM), which takes a portion of all municipal revenues and redistributes them on the basis of a fixed formula. The relatively modest amount of funds redistributed (13 percent of total municipal revenues in 1993), the relatively small weight assigned to municipal poverty or need in the formula, and the ability of municipalities to affect their own "need" status (which creates a moral hazard problem), make the FCM a weak and blunt means of redistribution (Marcel 1993). Varying tax bases probably explain a significant portion of the perceived differences in school quality across municipalities, including SIMCE standardized test results. These inequalities would probably be worse were it not for the misalignment of political and economic incentives mentioned above: if alcaldes in the wealthier communities experienced electoral pressure to improve their schools, if all or even most of their students came from the electorate in their *comuna*, they might be compelled to devote an even larger share of their municipality's resources to education.

Finally, the key element of Chilean post-welfare financing, the per-pupil subvention or the voucher, might not be well-matched to the education sector. First, per-student payments assume an economy of scale with the average and marginal costs assumed to fall down to a point and then rise. Schools in the private sector will take in students until the subvention value equals marginal cost. That economy of scale, while maximizing productive efficiency, might not be the school size associated with the most learning. The subvention mechanism, whatever the value of the subvention itself, contains a bias against small schools that, in the presence of competitive pressures and the absence of good measures of educational quality, will lead schools to grow and companies to establish chains of schools, which has already happened in Chile. That outcome might conflict with the goal of creating strong autonomous schools. Second, equal per-student payments provide a compelling incentive for schools to cut their costs by selecting the students that are easiest to educate. Like private health insurers, they find it cheaper to compete by enrolling most of the best students, or "creaming," than by improving the skills of the less gifted. In chapter 3, this study finds evidence suggesting that creaming is widespread in the Chilean subsidized sector.

Good Information

The rhetoric of decentralization suggests, even if the theoretical foundations of the post-welfare model do not, that it will promote participation in service delivery—voice for clients. And the post-welfare model assumes that the necessary information for exit pressures will be available, or if it is not, that the government will assume the responsibility to provide information because it is a public good. The Chilean experience in education raises serious questions about both of these assumptions.

Although little data is available, most observers agree that parents did not participate more in education as a result of the 1980 reforms. Given the extent of censorship, repression, and political disarticulation at the time, it would be surprising if they had. A number of decree laws in the years following the 1973 coup restricted allowable activities in and around schools, prescribed patriotic behavior on the part of students and teachers, and forbade "political" organizing in educational establishments.[39] One decree, which limited the function of parents' associations to "non-political" ends, also stated that those associations were entitled to see the school budget only "when the administration of the establishment determines it to be sanctioned in the law" (Decreto No. 632, February 20, 1982).

Beyond the authoritarian nature of the regime, however, other factors seem to have contributed to the absence of a noticeable increase in parental "voice." The ongoing centralist orientation in the Ministry of Education, in particular, which is itself embedded in the broader corporatism of Chilean politics and society, limited local initiative. Chilean law declares the existence of parents' associations and specifies their purposes, activities, and prerogatives. That tradition, in which the state and the political parties penetrate and organize nearly all aspects of civil society, does not easily accommodate a liberal or neoliberal framework that encourages individual initiative. The great majority of Chilean parents, for instance, even those whose children attend private schools, continue to believe that the ministry should remain dominant in education. (See the survey results in chapter 3.) Other sources of resistance to parental participation include the local hierarchies in municipal government and the teachers' union, which fears having to respond to the whims of uneducated parents. During the deliberations preceding the Estatuto Docente, for instance, the representative of the teachers' union opposed measures that would have granted parents an official role in evaluating teacher performance. There is also resistance to participation among parents themselves. Many of them have less education than their children and feel awkward expressing criticisms of schools. Although like parents everywhere they are often proud and supportive of their children's education, they can also resent it: it keeps children from work and introduces them to a world alien to their own.

How can parents who want to participate in their children's education determine whether a school is good? Most people rely on reputations. But these take time to form. And, particularly in Chile, they are frequently a simple function of the social class of a school's student population. Traditionally, parents would try to reach a little bit higher for their children's education, sending them to a municipality one rung up on the socioeconomic ladder. But with the housing relocation program of the military government, the overall decline in educational morale, and the new organization of the education sector, old signals of school quality were no longer as reliable. Getting good information grew more difficult at exactly the moment when it became more important.

Aware of this problem, the neoliberal designers of the Chilean system in 1982 created a standardized test, the Prueba de Evaluación del Rendimiento Escolar (PER), which eventually evolved into another test, Sistema de Medición de la Calidad de la Educación (SIMCE), which is administered nationally at grades four, eight, and ten. Although the test would presumably provide information on school quality to parents, its detailed results were not widely diffused because of resistance from teachers, who feared it would be misinterpreted. They argued that parents and politicians would blame teachers for low scores when in fact the social background of the students and low-level school inputs were more directly responsible for test outcomes. The ministry encountered the same problem when it tried to interpret the results itself. It used the test as a simultaneous measure of local needs and local performance, never deciding whether poorly performing schools should receive more resources (as a kind of targeting) or should be punished (by publicizing scores, leading to parental exit). Were poor scores a sign of a school's failure or an indication of the challenges it faced? Gonzalo Vial, the former minister of education, saw it as the latter, stating that a poorly performing municipality "could receive a technical service team from the Ministry that would go over like the fire fighters and help out" (Cox 1984, 155). On the other hand, neoliberals proposed a plan for merit pay in 1981 that would have rewarded high test scores, not low ones.

This points to a central problem in the post-welfare design for education. A market requires reliable information on school quality, but standardized tests usually do not measure and model exogenous components of educational achievement, such as parental and peer socioeconomic characteristics, and selection effects. Because they do not control for exogenous factors, there is usually no consensus about how to interpret discrepancies in test scores. In fact, controlling for selection effects in test analysis is an econometric problem of notorious difficulty. The ongoing controversies surrounding the Coleman report, which argued that private schools in the United States outperform public ones, illustrate how politically and technically thorny the problem remains (Coleman et al. 1982). Some schools systems, such as the Dallas Independent School District and the state of South Carolina in the United States, are developing testing systems that measure value added by schools and use a variety of adjustments to correct for their schools' populations (Clotfelter and Ladd 1996). But agreement on the relative performance of schools might only come with "dynamic, random assignment experiments over a number of years, with repeated measures of achievement" (Witte 1992, 391). Those experiments will initially be of limited generalizability and are not likely to happen any time soon. As a result, the post-welfare educational market will continue to suffer from information failures that seriously limit its promised efficiency gains.

Conclusions

The theories of public choice and educational choice contend that competitive forces can transform incentives in the public sector, making rewards to providers commensurate with their performance level. The theories do not explain, however, how service managers will determine which of their employees deserve higher salaries. Municipal mayors or education directors, even if their schools operate under hard budget constraints, might lack the capacity to evaluate teaching quality; and for a variety of reasons decentralized delivery systems might replicate hierarchical structures at the local level that weaken and disorganize the opinions of service recipients. Owners of privatized schools will find it difficult to assess the effect of a particular employee's performance on revenues because parents' choices are difficult to interpret and because reputations are sluggish. Educators and economists alike will contest the meaning of standardized test scores. Because stable relationships are important in the social sectors and because teachers are not easily replaced, threats of dismissal often will not be credible. Finally, the theories fail to acknowledge the existence of nonpecuniary incentives, such as professional morale, that weaken as the post-welfare model is applied.

A post-welfare model might fail to enhance incentives for other reasons. Providers will find it easier to lower costs by selecting their clients carefully than to raise revenues by improving service quality. The political incentive for municipalities to provide services will decline as the number of nonresidential clients increases. The existence of a parallel, privately funded sector will drain both the best professionals and political support from the publicly funded institutions.

The theories' account of interest groups, which organize to capture public sector agencies for their own benefit, simplifies the actual behavior of the state and professionals. The state often seeks to control social sector service delivery in order to guarantee public principles, such as fairness and the generality of citizenship, and to serve national goals such as macroeconomic equilibrium. Those goals in turn might benefit some groups, such as nativeborn residents and the financial sector, respectively, more than others. The state does protect the interests of service providers as well, of course; but which motive dominates is an empirical question. The Chilean experience illustrates that central government intervention can continue even when the regime views service providers antagonistically. Who captures what, moreover, is not clear. The weakness of the teaching profession, rooted in the limited nature of its technical autonomy, permits its domination from other sources, traditionally the state or political parties, occasionally the commercial sector. While public choice theory argues that educators wrest schools away from the families that schools are intended to serve, it misses a prior event: a variety of actors capture educational systems at the expense of the educators' interest in making schools conform to an educative end that they alone can supply.

Although underfunding, the authoritarian context, and inconsistent design were significant contributing factors, the application of the post-welfare model to Chilean education stumbled because it failed to take into account the specific characteristics of the sector. Because education shares many of those traits with other social sectors such as health care—particularly the difficulty in controlling for selection effects, the importance of stable relationships, the existence of ongoing interests in state intervention, a potential decline in professional morale, the misalignment of exit and voice, and shortcomings at the municipal level—this analysis demonstrates a set of general problems in the post-welfare model for the social sectors. A final potential criticism of the use of market forces in social sector service delivery, that they promote inequality, is examined in the next chapter.

Stratification in the Chilean Educational System

Systems of educational choice foster inequality, critics charge. They contend that when families choose schools, those with advantaged initial endowments will sort themselves into the best ones. Those schools soon become even better as students with advantages learn from one another, as their families contribute their own financial and political resources to their schools, as the schools draw teachers who want to work with that set of students, and as other schools and employers begin to recruit from them. Inequalities will accelerate if the system not only permits parents to choose schools but allows schools to select students. Concerns of this sort motivate many of the critics of educational choice, both in response to proposals in the United States and in the current subvention system in Chile.

Although showing that in a choice system schools that achieve highest also have more advantaged students would be consistent with the above story, evaluating inequality with a snapshot survey poses difficulties of interpretation. Such a demonstration, an empirically unsurprising result given the near universal correlation between school achievement and student family background in all systems of student allocation, choice or otherwise, might have several meanings. Because most studies find that family background explains a large part of school achievement, it will not be clear whether the higher achieving schools are in fact "better" (in that they would continue to achieve regardless of who their students were), whether their achievement is predicated upon having an advantaged student population, or both. If the higher achieving schools are not "better" in the first sense, however, then there will be no opportunity cost for students who do not attend them; and the charge of inequality leveled against a choice system, understood as school stratification by class or income, will have no moral weight because schools will be *wholly* passive vehicles for the reproduction of class. But everyone, both the rich and the poor, seems to behave as if the higher achieving schools are in fact "better." They probably believe that, even if a school's "value added" is small relative to family background, not studying with advantaged students might still carry an opportunity cost (there might be peer effects), and employers and other schools might well interpret attendance at higher achieving schools as a proxy for aptitude (there might be signaling effects). In either case, stratification becomes a morally relevant inequality in a system of school choice.

Given heterogeneity in student abilities and the existence of social classes, school stratification is unavoidable unless students are assigned to schools randomly (which is not the case anywhere). The policy question then becomes: which method of student allocation—by national exam, residence, or choice—is best? A national exam system might maximize the "sum total" of student achievement if peer effects are strong and if gifted students add more to each other's learning than their absence costs to classrooms of the less talented. It might be the most desirable method if one believes that it is more important for students at the top to obtain their potential than for students at the bottom. Residential and choice assignment might lead to more or less disparity among schools and among individuals than an exam-based system. It is difficult to know a priori. One method of examining the effects of the various allocation systems on equality would be to measure disparities among schools in different systems in relation to some baseline measure of inequality in the population, comparing the disparities in secondary education relative to primary education in two distinct systems, for instance. Another question of policy interest is whether different factors are associated with attending a "better" school in the different systems of student allocation; whether, for instance, being informed about school quality is in fact more valuable in a choice system than one based on residence.[1] The practice of ability-level tracking within schools, of course, raises related moral problems and complicates the ultimate research task by calling for work on within-school inequality.

Although it is limited to one system of student allocation in one country at a given point in time, the study included in this chapter seeks to advance the policy research agenda implied in the above paragraphs in a number of ways. First, it provides benchmark descriptive data on the Chilean "choice" or subvention system, data based on, to the author's knowledge, the most comprehensive existing survey of parental opinions, behaviors, and choices regarding education in Chile. Second, it provides a basis of preliminary comparison for studies of other countries and other systems of allocation. Third, it examines the Chilean system in its own right to determine whether certain policy interventions might reduce the inequalities persisting in or resulting from it.

Did the Choice System Improve Educational Performance in Chile?

An examination of the key education indicators, listed in table 1, is inconclusive.[2] Both overall enrollment and the gross enrollment rate in elementary education declined from 1981 to 1994. The drop in overall enrollment is largely attributable to a decline in the birth rate over this period, and the decline in gross enrollment is probably related to the slight decline in repetition rates, which reduced the fraction of students outside the six-to-fourteen age range in elementary school, and the recession of 1982–1983. The enrollment rate in secondary education increased from 65 percent to almost 80 percent over the period, which in turn is reflected in the rise in mean years of education in the population from 7.8 years in 1982 to 9.5 years in 1994. This gain, however, probably reflects the upward sloping long-term trend line in mean years of education in Chile, a consequence of the elementary school supply expansion in the 1960s and the increase in demand resulting from the rising returns to education that have accompanied Chile's economic modernization. Indeed, the mean years of education increased twice as much from 1970 to 1982, the period before the reform, than from 1982 to 1994.

The data on promotion rates show improvements from 1981 to 1994, with the figure for elementary education rising from 83.8 percent to 91.2 percent. This represents an improvement in the internal efficiency of the system but could be a symptom of lax standards as easily as of an improvement in quality: to reduce costs resulting from repetition, schools might be employing grade inflation.[3] The dropout rate declined noticeably in secondary education, and it improved dramatically at the elementary level, where it went from 8.1 percent in 1981 to 1.9 percent in 1994. Most of the decline in the dropout rate in elementary education occurred in 1982, when it fell to 2.7 percent. The explanation for this improvement might be related to the introduction of the new system, but it might also be a consequence of the declining wages and high unemployment that attended the deep recession of 1982–1983.

Evaluations of the Chilean "choice" system are complicated by the fact that steep cuts in funding for all levels of education accompanied the reforms. The value of the subvention declined 32 percent in real terms between the beginning of 1981 and November 1991 (Infante and Schiefelbein 1992). It recovered and exceeded its 1981 value only after the democratic government increased taxes for the sake of more education and health spending. Public expenditures on education as a percentage of GDP fell from 4.5 percent in 1981 to 2.9 percent in 1994. As a result, it is difficult to know

Table 1. Indicators of National Educational Achievement and Spending in Chile, 1981 and 1994

	1981	1994
Mean years of education	7.76[a]	9.47
Enrollment in elementary schools	2,139,319	2,088,508
Enrollment in secondary schools	554,749	664,498
Gross enrollment rate (%)		
Elementary	95.27[a]	93.29
Secondary	65.01[a]	79.72
Failure rate (%)		
Elementary	8.12	6.85
Secondary	12.68	12.27
Dropout rate (%)		
Elementary	8.06	1.92
Secondary	8.35	7.06
Promotion rate (%)		
Elementary	83.82	91.23
Secondary	78.97	80.67
Public expenditure on education		
In millions of pesos (1994)	360,672.40	448,124.90
As percentage of GDP	4.46	2.86
Public spending on higher education as percentage of public education budget	35.19[b]	18.47

Source: Ministerio de Educación, República de Chile, Compendio de Información Estadística, 1994.
   a. 1982 statistics.
   b. 1980 statistics.

whether the reasons for the absence of clear improvements in the key indicators, and for the widespread anecdotal accounts of the system's deteriora-
tion, result from problems in design or financing. Most establishments in the
subsidized sector in Chile operated two distinct half-day schools, a morning
shift and an evening shift, and many if not most teachers worked in two or
more institutions or had some other part-time job in order to make ends
meet. For most educators and most students, these conditions dominate and
mask the effects of the change to a "choice" system. In summary, it is impossible to know what the table 1 indicators would have looked like in the
absence of the reforms or had the reforms been adequately funded.

A handful of analyses base assessments of the Chilean system on the
results of a national standardized test, now called the SIMCE, which was
introduced in pilot form in 1982. The Ministry of Education has since then
administered the test in full form several times to students in the fourth and
eighth years of elementary school, and, in 1994, first tested students in their
second year of secondary school. Mean test scores in every sector have gradually improved from 1988 to 1994, which for some writers is proof of systemic improvement.[4] But the novelty of the test instrument and questions
concerning its consistency, the likelihood that instructors have learned to
"teach to the test," and the conflict of interest inherent in the fact that the
Ministry of Education administers a test that evaluates its own work all suggest that a more cautious interpretation is warranted. The existence of a
meaningful improvement in the 1980s, as well as its causes, are in doubt
(Cox 1997).

Other analysts, usually partisans of the "choice" system, point to the fact
that private subsidized schools consistently outperform municipal schools in
SIMCE results and claim, or sometimes imply, that this fact vindicates the
"choice" reforms because the more market-oriented sector, the one more "in
tune" with the broad purpose of the reforms, is doing better. But this view is
problematic. Several studies, including the results of the present analysis,
establish that the population of families in the private subsidized sector is on
average better endowed and more educated than families in municipal
schools (Aedo and Larrañaga 1994). This fact, and not the organizational
superiority of private schools, might explain their higher test scores; or the
effects of school organization might interact with the characteristics of the
families and students choosing them. In either case, the superior performance of the private subsidized sector depends on the existence of another
sector and on, in other words, their ability to "cream" the better students.
Like private health insurers, school owners might find it easier to compete by

creaming than by improving the quality of the services provided—in education creaming improves the apparent performance of an establishment not
only directly, via smarter and better endowed students, but indirectly,
through peer effects and interactions at the school.[5]

A few more statistically rigorous analyses attempt to control for the
socioeconomic differences between the municipal and private subsidized sectors, claiming that differences in sectoral test scores remain significant.
Rodríguez (1985) took a sample of 281 schools in Santiago and modeled
schools' average SIMCE scores as a linear function of parents' education,
teachers' experience, percentage of women teachers, the ratio of nonteacher
professionals to teachers, and a set of dummy variables for school sector. He
found that the coefficients on the dummies for private subsidized schools
were positive and statistically significant, as was the coefficient on the
dummy variable for municipal schools. (Public centralized schools, which
still existed at the time, were the base of comparison.) Rodríguez concluded
that the findings provided evidence supporting the decentralization and privatization policies of the military government.

Parry (1993) took a sample of about three thousand municipal and private subsidized schools in Chile and regressed average school SIMCE scores
on average parents' education, average socioeconomic level, school accessibility, the number of school-aged children per school in the municipality,
and two dummy variables for school sector. She found that while municipal
schools outperform private subsidized schools when parents have relatively
little education, private subsidized schools do better when parents are more
educated. All of the indicators these studies employ are school averages
because the ministry assembles no data, not even SIMCE scores, at the level
of the individual student. As a result, the analyses cannot control for student
abilities by constructing longitudinal studies (to get at value added), disag-
gregate the effects of socioeconomic status on test scores within a school, or
control for peer effects. The ministry's measure of school average socioeconomic status, moreover, is partly based on school characteristics, which
makes interpretations of its coefficient somewhat unclear.

The paucity of school input measures might be leading the writers to
interpret what are differences in the general characteristics of schools as differences in sectoral organization. And even if better data were available in
Chile and longitudinal measures of test scores at the individual level could
be constructed, the thorny issue of selection bias would remain: all of the
methodological controversies surrounding the Coleman reports are relevant
to the Chilean debate on municipal and private schools. Aedo and Larrañaga

(1994) address that problem by constructing a Mills ratio to fill in the truncated distributions in each sector. They then predict a test score gain on the order of 2–3 percent if an average student in the municipal sector were to switch to the private subsidized sector. Given the methodological controversies and the problems with the data, however, the significance and robustness of that estimate must be questioned.

Methodology and Data

Both the descriptive data and the estimation results in this study employ, for cross-tabs and the dependent variable, the category of "school type." It refers to a school's academic achievement level, determined by the school's average math score on the SIMCE. "Bottom" refers to schools with mean scores in the bottom third for the metropolitan region, "middling" to schools with mean scores in the middle third, and "top" to schools with scores in the upper third. Only the set of subsidized schools, which includes municipal, corporation, and private subsidized schools, is divided into types; the elite private schools are grouped together and are simply called "private paid." The SIMCE scores used for dividing schools into types are results from the fourth-year exam in 1992 in the case of elementary schools and the second-year exam of 1994 for secondary schools.[6]

One key question motivates this analysis: what factors are associated with a child attending a top school? A true model of educational choice would involve four theoretically separable events: (1) a family encounters a "choice set" when it enters the education market, (2) the family and the student apply to some of the schools in the choice set, (3) the child is accepted into some of those schools, and finally (4) the family selects a school from among those to which admission has been granted. Most of the household characteristics that influence search success would operate on more than one event in the process. High family income and advanced parental education, for example, might influence the choice set (so that it includes distant schools, schools with particular values or pedagogical orientation, or even private paid schools), might increase the likelihood of applying to more competitive schools, might enhance the student's chances of getting admitted, and might make it more likely that an accepted student in fact chooses a distant school. Similarly, valuing education highly would be associated with a more encompassing choice set, applying to more schools, enjoying higher odds of getting admission, and going to a good and distant school once admitted. In addition, a reciprocal causality problem arises with the importance placed on education: having gained her child's admission to a good school, a mother might then begin to value education more highly.

Measuring the separate effects of household characteristics on each of the four events is also methodologically problematic, particularly for the determination of a family's school choice set, which requires an aggregation of family values, school distance, tuition fees, and school quality in some meaningful way. Distinguishing the events is also time-consuming and cumbersome: it requires a survey instrument that reliably assesses the schools to which a student has applied and the acceptance or rejection decision at each school. The latter is especially difficult in a system like Chile's where the admission tests are frequently informal interviews with the student and/or the family, and where a rejection "decision" is expressed as a subtle suggestion to look elsewhere or a hint of "incompatibility" rather than a clear yes or no.

Because of these difficulties, the model below, which does not attempt to sort out the distinct events in the search process, is best understood not as a model of "choice," which would presumably include an enumeration of the various options available, but as a model of outcomes in the overall search process. The data available reveal the effects of household, school, and child characteristics on the combined outcome of the four events. While some of the variables, such as family income, enter into the true model in all events and in a complicated fashion, others, such as a mother's search techniques, probably enter into a single event (in this case event 2).

Moreover, family income and the other socioeconomic variables pose an additional problem for the analysis: these are related not only to search success but also to the schools' achievement scores. The students' family backgrounds are in all likelihood correlated with their individual test scores and therefore to their schools' average test scores, which are the measure of the schools' achievement status, or their type. The more homogenous a school in the family background of its students, the higher will be the correlation between a random student's family background and the school's average SIMCE score. Hence, the correlation between household socioeconomic traits and school SIMCE scores will be strong for schools with particularly high or low scores: bottom and top schools. One way to resolve this endogeneity problem is to estimate the contribution of family background to a school's test scores, but this requires individual-level achievement scores, which are not available in Chile. When interpreting the results below, then, it will be useful to consider the socioeconomic background traits a composite of search variables and cultural capital contributions to the school test score, a composite whose presence in the estimations controls for familial contribution to school achievement and thus permits the remaining variables to be interpreted as estimators of search success in the choice system.

An ideal experiment would have modeled the influence of the explanatory variables prospectively, before families choose schools, because the outcome of the search process might affect some of the ex post measures of attitudes and behaviors. Further research should certainly explore prospective measures where possible.

The source of the data is a door-to-door survey conducted in Greater Santiago during December 1993 and January 1994. In the selected households, data were collected for every child attending an elementary or secondary school in the previous year. The interviewee was always the mother, the father, or the guardian; and she was most often the mother (77.4 percent of the households), since mothers generally manage the education of children in Chile. The sampling method consisted of a simple random sample without clusters or strata. The sample size was 726 households. In those households, 1,221 students had attended elementary or secondary school during the previous academic year. The multinomial logit estimates used all students in the subsidized sector with nonmissing data, which reduced the sample size to 850 students.

The sampling method consisted of a simple random sample, without clusters or strata, whose frame relied on the "Census of Population and Housing" of April 1982, the "pre-census" of 1992, and aerial photographs from the national air force. The first and only unit of selection was the household. If no one was present in a selected household or if the desired subject was busy, the interviewers returned a maximum of three times to the locale. At that point, the household was replaced by another one from the area.

The size of the sample was 726 households, in which there were 1,221 children studying in elementary or secondary schools. As table 2 shows, of these students, 520 (42.6 percent) were attending private subsidized schools, 490 (40.1 percent) were in the municipal sector, 181 (14.8 percent) in the private paid sector, and 30 (2.5 percent) in corporation schools. The sectoral breakdown of the sample compares well with the official ministry figures for the metropolitan area in 1992: 40.1 percent municipal, 45.5 percent private subsidized, 12.0 percent private paid, and 2.4 percent corporation. In the sample, 924 students (75.7 percent) were in elementary school and 297 students (24.3 percent) in secondary. Official statistics for 1992 indicate that 73.9 percent of enrolled students in the metropolitan area were in elementary school and 26.1 percent in secondary.

Table 2. The 1,221 Students in the Sample, by School Level, Sector, and Type

	n	(%)
By level of schooling		
Elementary	924	(75.7)
Secondary (scientific-humanistic)	172	(14.1)
Secondary (vocational)	125	(10.2)
By sector		
Private subsidized	520	(42.6)
Municipal	490	(40.1)
Private paid	181	(14.8)
Corporation	30	(2.5)
By school type[a]		
Bottom	342	(33.3)
Middling	408	(39.8)
Top	276	(26.9)
Private paid	181	(15.0)

By school type and level,[a] with column frequencies

	Elementary		Secondary (scientific-humanistic)		Secondary (vocational)	
	n	(%)	n	(%)	n	(%)
Bottom	259	(28.3)	28	(15.6)	55	(48.2)
Middling	296	(32.4)	60	(33.5)	52	(45.6)
Top	230	(25.2)	39	(21.8)	7	(6.1)
Private paid	129	(14.1)	52	(29.1)	0	(0)

By school type and sector, with column frequencies[a]

	Municipal		Private Subsidized		Private Paid		Corporation	
	n	(%)	n	(%)	n	(%)	n	(%)
Bottom	227	(46.9)	108	(21.1)	3	(1.7)	7	(33.3)
Middling	177	(36.6)	212	(41.4)	6	(3.4)	19	(39.8)
Top	80	(16.5)	192	(37.5)	170	(95.0)	4	(26.9)

Source: Author.

a. For schools with SIMCE scores.

Breaking down school sector and level by school type is illustrative. Whereas 95 percent of the students in the sample who attend private paid schools are in tòp private paid schools, only 38 percent of students in the private subsidized sector are in top schools, and just 17 percent in the municipal sector. This reflects the fact that private subsidized schools as a group outperform the municipal sector. The figure also shows that students in subsidized scientific-humanistic schools are far more likely to be in a top school than students in subsidized vocational schools, with a probability of 30.1 percent and 6.1 percent, respectively. In general, vocational schools exhibit lower levels of achievement than scientific-humanistic schools.

Given that the sampling area was restricted to Greater Santiago, the survey results can be generalized to the country as a whole only with strong qualifications. Parents in many rural areas enjoy little or no choice in their selection of schools, and most establishments in their choice sets are municipally managed one-room schoolhouses. Because more than 80 percent of the Chilean population reside in urban areas, however, the results from Santiago are probably not a terrible first approximation of the functioning of the "choice" system in the nation as a whole.

A Model of the Factors that Contribute to Search Success

Table 3 presents mean values for a number of socioeconomic variables by school type. (See the appendix for an extended analysis of the descriptive statistics and for comparisons of the results across sectors as well as across school types.) Even a cursory glance at table 3 is enough to discern the pattern: students in higher achieving schools pay more for their education, are more likely to have taken a test to enroll in their present school, come from households with more income and greater assets, and have parents who are more informed about school quality and who are more likely to choose schools for academic reasons. These several advantages appear correlated with search success. Table 3 also establishes the existence of widespread student testing in the Chilean subsidized sector: the overall rate of testing in the subsidized sector is 28 percent, which is extremely high given that these tests, although not formally illegal, are culturally and normatively proscribed and that the great majority of school principals would deny administering them. The appendix describes, in addition, the low level of information regarding school quality that parents exhibit; and it demonstrates that students in higher achieving schools travel farther to get to school, spend more time and money in transportation, and pay more in fees than students in bottom and middling schools.

A number of the measures that vary consistently across school types are likely to be correlated with one another. The use of specific indicators to determine school quality and a father's having attended college, for instance, have a correlation coefficient of $\rho = 0.15$. To determine which variables affect the likelihood of being enrolled in a good school independent of the effects of other variables, results from multinomial logit estimations are presented in tables 4 and 5.

The two models presented in tables 4 and 5 list results for both the equation comparing top and bottom schools and the equation comparing the odds of attending middling and bottom schools. The comparison between top and bottom schools is more useful for the purposes of this analysis, however, because the difference in achievement between the school types is clearer: whereas schools with SIMCE scores in the 32nd and 34th percentiles, categorized as bottom and middling schools, respectively, are comparable in quality, the differences between schools in the 70th and 30th percentiles are so large that they can be considered different kinds of schools.

The variables in tables 4 and 5 are grouped into four types: socioeconomic, behavioral, attitudinal, and those unrelated to families. In general, the estimations find that a higher socioeconomic background characterizes students who enroll in higher achieving schools. They also demonstrate that some parental behaviors or orientations, in particular being informed about school quality, using specific indicators to assess school quality, and choosing a school for academic reasons, are associated with attendance in more accomplished schools. Finally, the estimations find that attitudes concerning the importance of education are not correlated with attending higher achieving schools, with the significant exception of a sense of entitlement with respect to school choice, measured by responses to the hypothetical loss of the right to choose a school.

Model 2 adds two socioeconomic, three behavioral, six attitudinal, and two other variables to the predictors in model 1. The overall likelihood-ratio chi-square comparing the two models is χ^2 (26 d.f.) = 25.81. Both the Wald tests on the individual variables and the likelihood-ratio chi-square tests on the four groups of variables indicate that these additions do not significantly add to the predictive power of model 1. One of the variables added in model 2 is residing in a municipality with a high concentration (40 percent or more) of top schools. Its inclusion is meant to ascertain whether the socioeconomic background and behavioral variables are proxies for an underlying

Table 3. Characteristics of Students' Families, by School Achievement Level

	Bottom n=342	Middling n=408	Top n=276	Privately Paid n=181
Household per capita income (pesos per month)[a][b][c]	21,563 (19,985) [n=335]	28,336 (27,291) [n=401]	39,663 (30,111) [n=258]	157,347 (130,509) [n=142]
Mother's education (years)[b]	7.8 (3.2) [n=338]	9.3 (3.2) [n=404]	10.6 (3.3) [n=277]	14.8 (3.1) [n=176]
Father's education (years)[b]	8.7 (3.6) [n=297]	9.8 (3.0) [n=344]	11.3 (3.3) [n=255]	15.7 (3.1) [n=171]
Family reads an "elite" newspaper (%)[b]	4.7	11.3	19.2	77.9
Family owns car (%)[b]	0.9	2.9	9.1	51.3
Family would be "very angry" or "upset" if they lost the right to choose a school (%)[b]	53.5	53.7	71.4	93.3
Family chose school primarily for nonacademic reasons (%)[b]	58.2	49.0	32.6	13.8
Child took a test to enroll in the present school (%)[b]	15.4 [n=337]	27.6 [n=402]	46.1 [n=271]	81.8 [n=181]
Total payments to school (in 1993 pesos)[a][b][c]	9,319 (12,075)	13,818 (18,261)	25,223 (36,635)	624,330 (352,535)
As fraction of household income	0.010	0.011	0.013	0.096
Family could name two subsidized schools in the metropolitan region whose test scores were in the upper third for the region (%)[b]	26.3	38.4	56.9	53.0

Source: Author.

Note: Standard deviations are in parentheses. Subsample sizes in brackets are exceptions. Here and in following tables, the word *family* denotes either parents or guardians.

a. In 1993, 400 Chilean pesos = US$1.

b. Mean values are significantly different for bottom and top schools, at p < .05.

c. Means test employed a logarithmic transformation of the variable.

Table 4. The Relative Odds of Attending a Top, Middling, or Bottom School, Model 1

Independent Variable	Log[Pr(top)/ Pr(bottom)]	Odds Ratio	Log[Pr (middling)/ Pr(bottom)]	Odds Ratio
Household per capita income	0.622 (0.163)	1.864	0.410 (0.137)	1.507
Mother's education				
Some secondary	1.178 (0.251)	3.245	0.931 (0.197)	2.538
Some higher	1.448 (0.626)	4.254	0.936 (0.611)	2.545
Father's education				
Some secondary	−0.002 (0.260)	0.998	0.068 (0.198)	1.071
Some higher	0.459 (0.516)	1.583	−0.800 (0.557)	0.449
Family owns car	1.984 (0.772)	7.273	0.719 (0.801)	2.052
Parents are married	0.791 (0.412)	2.206	−0.043 (0.271)	0.958
Family are informed about school quality	0.652 (0.225)	1.919	0.203 (0.195)	1.225
Family chose school for nonacademic reasons	−0.739 (0.412)	0.478	−0.208 (0.179)	0.812
Family attended all parents' association meetings	0.499 (0.232)	1.645	0.274 (0.186)	1.316
Family used specific indicators in school search	0.756 (0.406)	2.131	0.208 (0.399)	1.231
Family would be "very angry" if lost right to choose school	0.423 (0.226)	1.526	−0.289 (0.178)	0.749
Child took a test to enroll in school	1.219 (0.248)	3.381	0.798 (0.225)	2.222

Source: Author.

Note: Asymptotic standard errors are in parentheses. N = 850: bottom, 286; middling, 331; top, 233. The equations include a constant. The base group for parental education consists of parents with no secondary schooling. Car ownership is determined by whether the child commuted to school in the family car. A high concentration of top schools is defined as over 40 percent.

predictor of region of residence or municipal wealth (which is associated with the number of top schools a municipality possesses). While the regional variable does not add to the overall predictive power of the model and the Wald test for its significance in the top/bottom equation cannot be rejected, both the Wald test and the likelihood ratio test (not shown) find it significant in the middling/bottom equation. This finding, consistent with the remainder of the estimation results, suggests that while attending a top-tier school in the subsidized sector is associated with specific parental attitudes and behaviors, attending a middle-level school is more of a casual event, related more to the region of residence than to family dispositions. Three other variables that just barely failed Wald tests at the 5 percent level, living with married parents, using specific indicators in a school search, and valuing the right to choose a school, were jointly significant: the likelihood-ratio chi-square was χ^2 (6 d.f.) = 22.65.

A number of household socioeconomic traits, including income, are highly significant predictors of top school attendance. The gender of the head of the household was of interest because of the hypothesis that after adjusting for household income, households with females at their head would be more likely to provide a better education for their children because women are more in tune with the educational needs of their children and can act on this knowledge more forcefully if they are in charge. This turned out not to be the case. Children with mothers who attended college, however, were 4.3 times more likely to attend a top school than children whose mothers had no secondary education; and children with mothers having attended some secondary school were 2.3 times as likely. This conforms to findings in other studies that have emphasized the exceptional importance of mother's education for the child's welfare. The two variables for father's (or male guardian's) education, while not significant when taken alone, jointly contribute to the model: the joint likelihood-ratio chi-square test "father some secondary education" and "father some higher education" was χ^2 (4 d.f.) = 12.09. Family car ownership, a measure of wealth assessed using the proxy of whether a child in the family commuted to school in a car belonging to the family, made children six times more likely to attend a top school.[7] Living with married parents or married guardians meant that a child was more than twice as likely to attend a top school than a bottom school. As mentioned above, the significance of socioeconomic predictors might indicate success at any stage of the search process, or it might reflect the increased contribution of a child to the cultural capital of a school. In either case, the results establish a surprising degree of class-based differentiation even within the subsidized sector: socioeconomic variables predict top school attendance more strongly than behaviors and attitudes.

The results on parental behaviors offer useful insights into the Chilean "choice" system in education and the mechanisms by which students enroll in the better subsidized schools. Students whose parents are informed about school quality are 1.9 times more likely to enroll in top schools than in bottom schools, controlling for socioeconomic and other characteristics. Note that this effect is predicated upon the current, poor level of information among consumers. One can assume that if the overall level of information in the population were to increase, the costs of being uninformed, and the magnitude of the coefficient on the information predictor, would increase to an even higher level. This finding should offer a sound reason to make SIMCE results readily available to all parents: knowing about school quality gives parents, even the relatively poor and less educated, an effective resource in the struggle to provide the best available education for their children. The model also shows that certain search techniques increase the relative odds of attending a top school: children of parents who use specific indicators to assess school quality are more than twice as likely to be enrolled in top schools, while those with parents who have chosen schools for nonacademic reasons are less than half as likely to do so. These search techniques should also be emphasized and encouraged in the ministry's official campaigns. While a parental disposition to attend meetings is important in predicting top school attendance, other participation measures, such as volunteering in school and speaking to teachers, are not. The interpretation of the significance on meeting attendance should be cautious because while being predisposed to attend meetings might contribute to a more vigorous school search, attending a top school might in turn encourage meeting attendance. The survey question did not ask interviewees how often they attended meetings in past years or in other schools because the reliability of that information seemed questionable.

The model finds that the value attached to the liberty to choose a school is an exception to the general result that attitudes are not good predictors of type of school attended. If an interviewee felt very strongly about the importance of "choice," her child was 1.5 times more likely to attend a top school than a bottom school. This suggests that while the extent to which parents value education relative to other goods is not critical in the search process, some feeling of prerogative or entitlement, which would presumedly be associated with parental income and education but whose effect is independent of them, leads parents to success in the search. This result also supports the

Table 5. The Relative Odds of Attending a Top, Middling, or Bottom School, Model 2

Independent Variable	Log[Pr(top)/ Pr(bottom)]	Odds Ratio	Log[Pr (middling)/ Pr(bottom)]	Odds Ratio
Household per capita income	0.560 (0.174)	1.750	0.319 (0.144)	1.376
Mother's education				
Some secondary	1.157 (0.259)	3.179	0.882 (0.202)	2.414
Some higher	1.429 (0.643)	4.173	0.908 (0.628)	2.470
Father's education				
Some secondary	−0.044 (0.265)	0.957	0.056 (0.202)	1.058
Some higher	0.396 (0.535)	1.486	−0.934 (0.587)	0.393
Family owns car	2.076 (0.777)	7.971	0.797 (0.805)	2.219
Parents are married	1.278 (0.488)	3.581	0.266 (0.320)	1.305
Female-headed household[a]	1.000 (0.527)	2.722	0.537 (0.406)	1.711
Family reads "elite" newspaper[a]	0.215 (0.390)	1.240	0.308 (0.359)	1.362
Family are informed about school quality	0.600 (0.233)	1.821	0.128 (0.204)	1.136
Family chose school for nonacademic reasons	−0.725 (0.227)	0.484	−0.189 (0.185)	0.828
Family attended all parents' association meetings	0.474 (0.245)	1.606	0.208 (0.196)	1.231
Family used specific indicators in school search	0.752 (0.424)	2.122	0.220 (0.416)	1.245
Family considered other schools in search[b]	0.336 (0.271)	1.399	0.107 (0.238)	1.113
Family volunteered at school[b]	−0.159 (0.229)	0.853	−0.266 (0.192)	0.767

Table 5. *(Continued)*

Independent Variable	Log[Pr(top)/ Pr(bottom)]	Log[Pr Odds Ratio	Log (middling)/ Pr(bottom)]	Odds Ratio
No. of times family spoke to teacher or principal[b]	−0.002 (0.013)	0.998	0.006 (0.010)	1.006
Family would be "very angry" if lost right to choose school	0.409 (0.235)	1.505	−0.333 (0.186)	0.717
Family believe ministry should manage schools[c]	−0.177 (0.289)	0.838	0.164 (0.243)	1.179
Family believe education is:				
More important than a job[c]	−0.023 (0.279)	0.977	−0.085 (0.235)	0.918
More important than money[c]	0.233 (0.290)	1.263	0.262 (0.242)	1.299
More important than religion[c]	−0.260 (0.235)	0.771	−0.183 (0.196)	0.832
More important than ethnicity[c]	0.139 (0.244)	1.149	0.081 (0.206)	1.084
More important than a place to to live[c]	0.117 (0.251)	1.124	0.484 (0.206)	1.621
Child took a test to enroll in school	1.119 (0.255)	3.289	0.776 (0.231)	2.173
Region has high concentration of top schools[d]	0.794 (0.628)	2.212	1.234 (0.590)	3.457
Family believe their child is academically "above average"[d]	0.241 (0.306)	1.273	−0.007 (0.214)	0.993

Source: Author.

Note: Asymptotic standard errors are in parentheses. N = 850: bottom, 286; middling, 331; top, 233. The equations include a constant. The base group for parental education consists of parents with no secondary schooling. Car ownership is determined by whether the child commuted to school in the family car. A high concentration of top schools is defined as over 40 percent.

a. Joint likelihood chi-square χ^2 (4 d.f.) = 4.57.
b. Joint likelihood chi-square χ^2 (6 d.f.) = 3.75.
c. Joint likelihood chi-square χ^2 (12 d.f.) = 12.02.
d. Joint likelihood chi-square χ^2 (12 d.f.) = 12.02.

position that officials should encourage and publicize the prerogative to choose among parents. In the middling/bottom equation, this sense of entitlement was not significant but another attitudinal variable, the importance of a place to live relative to the importance of education, was. Because a good place to live was the good most favored relative to education among middling parents, this suggests that an extremely high value placed on education increases the odds of attending a middling school relative to a bottom school, but that success in attending an above-average subsidized school relies on search skills or socioeconomic background more than attitudes. This might explain the helplessness some disadvantaged families feel: no matter how much they value education, the doors to the top subsidized schools depend on social class and on skills they might not know how to attain. Valuing education gets one only so far in the search process.

A child's having taken a test to enroll in his or her present school was strongly associated with top school attendance. Cross-tabulations between a child's having taken an admission test and his or her mother's having attended college, between admissions testing and a father's having attended college, and between admissions testing and family car ownership found that all subsidized sector students in the sample from the higher levels of socioeconomic background and who took admissions tests were attending top schools. Meanwhile the coefficient on a child possessing above-average academic abilities as reported by parents, as well as an interaction between having taken a test and the child possessing above-average academic abilities, is not significant in either of the models. These results are consistent with the interpretation that the exams, as is widely believed, are not merely diagnostic but are used for selection. They also suggest that schools use parental background in place of (or as a proxy for) a child's academic potential. That the reported academic ability of the child is not significant suggests that parents do not search harder for children that they believe to be academically capable—once again, motivation is not as important as search skills. Another child-related trait, student gender, barely varied across school types, was found to be very insignificant in the preliminary logit estimates, and was not included in the first model.

Variables relating to school expenditures and transportation costs were not included in any of the models because, although they seemed to vary noticeably by school type (see table 14, appendix), they are better understood as ex post facto measures of what a family expends to get their child to the chosen school than as properties of all the top schools in the families' choice set during the search process. Another way of handling payments and transportation costs—treating them as prices in the estimation of a demand equation—would require combining prices and school test scores into a single measure, as well as sorting out the separate effects of a student's contribution to a school test score and the attractiveness of a school's achievement level to a student, in ways that remain both practically difficult and theoretically implausible. The fact that gaining admission into top schools seems to require greater resources, as tables 8 and 14 suggest, should be captured in the model by the coefficient on household income.[8]

Because the multinomial logit is a nonlinear estimation, the coefficients in tables 4 and 5 do not tell us whether any given child will be more or less likely to attend a top school than another. Table 6 presents a more useful interpretation of the multinomial logit coefficients. The numbers represent the increments in the percent probability of a child's attending a top school given the stated hypothetical changes. In each case, the increment is the difference between a baseline probability of attending a top school and the prediction obtained when the coefficients from model 1 are applied to the hypothetical change. In the case of per capita income, the baseline is calculated by averaging the individuals' probabilities of attending a top school using the original values in the sample, and the new probabilities result from applying the model 1 coefficients to across-the-board increases in household per capita income of $10,000 pesos and $25,000 pesos. In the case of the categorical variables, the baseline assumes that all individuals in the sample are of one category (uninformed about school quality, for instance), and the hypothetical change then places all individuals in the other category (informed about school quality). The increments are then the means of the differences in the individual probabilities before and after the hypothetical changes. It should be noted that these increments are means only and that the distributions of the increments among individuals might well differ greatly across explanatory variables.[9]

The results in table 6 show that while substantial increases in household income would increase the average probability of attending a top school between 2 percent and 4 percent, having parents who attend college would increase the probability by much more, over 14 percent. It is interesting to note that while secondary education appears critical for mothers, in the case of fathers it is college education that significantly enhances the odds that a child will attend an above-average subsidized school. One interpretation of this difference is that a father's college education is a proxy for permanent household income, but a mother's secondary education improves the child's education directly through her influence on and management of her children's education. A substantial increase in family assets, measured by a family car, increases the probability of top school attendance by over 27 percent, and living with married parents raises the probability by 11 percent. The above-mentioned qualifications regarding endogeneity apply to these estimates as well: socioeconomic variables probably increase the odds of top school attendance both by improving the chances of search success and by contributing to the cultural capital of the school.

The estimates in table 6 also find that certain parental dispositions, including strong beliefs about the right to choose a school, using specific indicators to assess school quality, choosing a school for academic reasons, and being informed about school quality will each independently raise the probability of top school attendance by 8–10 percent. Attending all meetings of the parents' association raises the probability by about 5 percent. These figures suggest that socioeconomic background does not overwhelm these contributing factors to search success, and that there is room for policy innovations to encourage those parental dispositions found to contribute to children's attendance in the better schools. It should be noted, however, that

Table 6. Factors Affecting the Probability of Attending a Top School

Increase in household per capita income[a]	
10,000 pesos per month	+2.2
25,000 pesos per month	+4.5
Increase in mother's education	
Some secondary	+9.5
Some higher	+14.2
Increase in father's education	
Some secondary	–0.7
Some higher	+14.8
Family owns car	+27.4
Child lives with married parents	+11.0
Family are informed about school quality	+8.2
Family chose school for nonacademic reasons	–9.3
Family used specific indicators in school search	+10.3
Family would be "very angry" if lost right to choose school	+9.3
Family attended all parents' association meetings	+4.8

Source: Author.

Note: The probabilities are evaluated using individual data. The base group for parental education consists of parents with no secondary schooling. Car ownership is determined by whether the child commuted to school in the family car.

a. In 1993 pesos: 400 Chilean pesos = US$1.

these estimates are for marginal changes only—large-scale changes would run up against dynamic interactions among the variables, which this analysis does not attempt to model, against the obvious supply constraints on top school attendance, and against other possible obstacles to egalitarian education, such as the screening functions of education.

These multinomial logit models assume that the family effects on the odds of attending a particular school type for two siblings are identical to those on the odds for two noncohabiting, unrelated students with identical household characteristics: in other words, there are no intrafamily effects among siblings, or equivalently, if such effects exist the observed variables capture them all. If there are unmeasured intrafamily effects, these will not only lead to underestimated standard errors (due to the introduction of clustering into the sample design) but biased estimators. This problem is generic to sample designs of this sort, and there are no standard statistical corrections. But given the small size of the clusters, about 1.7 students per household (this does not vary significantly across school types), the effect of intrafamily correlations on the estimation results is probably not fatal. In addition, because the sample provides an unbiased estimate of the number of students per household in the population, and because intrafamily effects influence outcomes in that population—they are not merely an artifact of the sampling design—it can be argued that those effects are captured in the model utilized, and that an estimation that isolated students from their siblings would in fact misrepresent the environment of the true population.[10]

Conclusions

This chapter reports several findings concerning the system of educational choice in Chile. First, households with higher socioeconomic status are substantially more likely to enroll their children in schools exhibiting higher levels of achievement than households of lesser means. The findings confirm that the social and economic chasm between the subsidized sector and the private paid sector remains enormous, and they establish the existence of substantial divisions within the subsidized choice system. They show that previous work, by focusing exclusively on differences between the municipal and private subsidized sectors and ignoring differences among school types, underestimates the degree of stratification in the Chilean system. Second, information, valuing the right to choose a school, and a search technique that uses specific indicators of school quality are shown (net of socioeconomic differences) to be associated with a student attending a high-achieving school. The choice system appears to reward those families who inform themselves, who know what to look for in a good school, and who feel entitled to their right to choose. This result is consistent with findings on the choice system in other settings (Witte and Rigdon 1992). Third, the survey presents evidence consistent with the existence of widespread admissions testing in the subsidized sector and finds a significant relationship between a school's testing policies and its level of achievement. It is safe to say that creaming accounts for at least a portion of the variation in achievement levels among subsidized schools. Fourth, families whose children attend higher achieving schools tend to pay more for attending them, travel farther to reach them, and utilize more expensive means of transport to and from school. The choice system appears to reward families whose choice sets are more expansive. Finally, although families in schools at all levels of achievement seem to value education and would be willing to multiply their education expenses several fold for the opportunity to attend an outstanding school (see the appendix), few parents are genuinely informed about school quality and most continue to believe in the efficacy of central authorities.

The explanation for that lag in parental dispositions might be that parents rationally choose to stay uninformed given the paucity of real alternatives available to them and the overall low level of school quality, that education is a distinctive good whose quality is known and measured with inherent subjectivity, or that institutional transformation is a slow process entailing very gradual shifts in the cognitive framework of those involved. If parents remain relatively uninformed for rational reasons, the contradictions and incoherencies in the system described in the previous chapter are preventing the choice system from realizing potential gains in efficiency and are also perhaps contributing to inequality by permitting family background to play an unusually strong role in student allocation. Although correcting those contradictions is an obvious policy prescription, the next two chapters demonstrate that deeply rooted political and structural factors make them difficult to eliminate.

The Politics of Post-Welfare Reforms in Education

The "Washington consensus" notwithstanding, very few countries have reformed their social sectors along the lines of the post-welfare model. Those that have attempted to do so have encountered political resistance that blocked, limited, or transformed the reform efforts. In some cases, the result was an incoherent policy design whose incentives are arguably even worse than before. Understanding the political dynamics of those reforms will help to illuminate what is politically possible and will help analysts determine whether proposed changes are likely to succeed. It will also illustrate the ways in which political ideas have embedded themselves in organizations and institutions, making clearer the arguments for and against post-welfare reforms.

Because the post-welfare attack targets the incentives of service providers and the ways in which teachers and medical personnel "capture" the benefits of programs for themselves, it is no surprise that organized service providers usually present the most concerted resistance. The post-welfare model would threaten the job stability they enjoy as civil servants. It would link their income to their performance, subjecting them to a kind of scrutiny to which they are unaccustomed. Further, it would threaten the existence of their unions by forcing them to negotiate individually or collectively with multiple small employers, whether municipalities or private for-profit providers.

Some rational choice theories predict that reform efforts will encounter collective action problems: interest groups will mobilize to block changes in service delivery more effectively than consumers will organize to promote them. This kind of account of social sector politics and policy is forceful for Chile, where public sector unions have been an important actor in domestic politics for most of the twentieth century and have often captured key posts in the ministries of health and education. Every democratically appointed minister of health, for example, had been a doctor until 1989. Similarly, regional directors of the education ministry were officials from the teachers' unions more frequently than not.

Although the interest group account of the political economy of social sector service is useful, it needs to be supplemented with a detailed description of political opportunities and institutional constraints. The variation in reform outcomes across countries and across time suggests that no mechanistic or "black box" account of interest group influence will do. Rather, the particular political institutions of a country, including its constitutional structures, formal and informal practices of political parties, and the electoral system—the "rules of the game"—affect the outcome of policy reform efforts (Immergut 1992).

This chapter argues that the military regime succeeded in implementing the reforms because the authoritarian climate and the regime's repressive strategies disarticulated the resistance that would have been expected in a pluralist setting. The chapter also contends, however, that divisions among policy-making elites in the military regime and relative indifference to education as such at the highest level of the regime led to contradictions in its post-welfare policy design. Although a certain type of "strong" or "autonomous" authoritarianism might be more effective than democracy at implementing neoliberal economic reforms and particular strategies of capital accumulation (Collier 1979; Haggard 1990), openness and public debate is crucial for the effective transformation of incentives in a sector that, like education, involves so many providers and clients, requires by its nature a decentralized form of service delivery, and depends critically on habits and traditions that are deeply embedded. The chapter then examines educational policy making in the first few years of the democratic government, again focusing exclusively on the question of the regime's stance toward the post-welfare or neoliberal incentive structures. It identifies some confusion in both the ideology and the practice of the government's policies and traces the causes of the contradictions and policy reversals to the specific trajectory of the government's actions, to the influence of the teachers' union on the opposition parties, to increasing militancy and divisions in the teachers' union, and to changes in the democratic government's political leadership.

The Relative Autonomy of the Military Regime

The neoliberal social sector reforms went farther in Chile than in other countries because of the strength of the Chilean regime's ideological commitment and because of the degree of its autonomy from civil society, the government bureaucracies, and the political parties.[1] The organizations and interest groups that would fight ideologically driven government initiatives in pluralist societies were silent.[2] The military junta itself was highly unified, resembling a dictatorship more closely than the other military governments of the region. Although Pinochet's lack of interest in the details of education policy, relative to his other concerns, permitted some disagreement among policy-making elites in the education sector, including statist expressions, the overall direction and the rhetorical tone of the reforms was never in doubt. This section describes the regime's political repression in the education sector, demonstrating how that freed it to impose neoliberal reforms.

Although it seemed at first that the military regime would be short-lived, lasting just long enough to restore order to a chaotic and hypermobilized polity, it soon became apparent that military hardliners, the secret police, and some influential civilians advocated indefinite military rule. As the internal repression mounted, the junta developed the view that the cause of the nation's decay had not only been Marxism but the inability of the nation's democratic institutions—political parties, Congress, and unions—to resist it. Extirpating the communist presence would require not just coercion but an institutional transformation.

Among the first political institutions the military regime abolished were the municipalities. Congress was also disbanded, as were the political parties and the unions. In education, the junta suspended the payment of membership dues to the principal education workers union, the Sindicato Unico de Trabajadores de la Educación (SUTE), and froze the union's assets, on December 11, 1973. One year later, with Decree Law 1284, the union and all other teachers' organizations were dissolved.

Although high-level Ministry of Education officials from the Allende regime were forced into exile, the junta did not replace many midlevel ministry civil servants: despite the extraconstitutional nature of the coup, the junta sought to gain legitimacy by respecting Chilean laws such as the Estatuto Administrativo governing the dismissal of civil servants. The regime circumvented the usual governmental procedures, however, by vesting decision-making power in governmental bodies it trusted. For the social sectors, a group of like-minded neoliberal economists in the Office of Planning and Development (ODEPLAN) would lead the design of policies from 1974 to 1982; and the Office of the Budget in the Ministry of Finance (DIRPRES) would do the same from 1982 to 1985 or so, when significant powers would be restored to the Ministry of Education itself.

In 1973 the junta quickly occupied the educational institutions in the country. The air force took control of the University of Chile, the navy assumed command of the Catholic University, and the army of the State Technical University. The new rector of the University of Chile parachuted down to the campus, as if landing in enemy territory. The junta proceeded to replace top-level educational supervisors throughout the country, including the minister, the ministry's chief directors, allegedly Marxist faculty members, the university rectors, and a significant fraction, perhaps a majority, of the some six thousand school principals in the country. Thousands of teachers and midlevel officials in the ministry suspected of socialist or communist ties or leftist leanings were fired. Hundreds of centrist and leftist faculty left universities for independent research centers or exile. Naval admirals Hugo Castro Jiménez, Arturo Troncoso, and Luis Niemann Núñez Daroch headed the ministry for the first five years. The junta suspended semiautonomous bodies tied to the ministry, such as the National Council of Education, the National Association of Nursery Schools, and the Center for Pedagogical Training, Experimentation, and Research, and vested their powers in the high-level division chiefs, who were often military officials (Núñez 1984; Gajardo 1982; Bermudez 1975).

The junta also moved quickly to rewrite curricula and to control daily activities in schools. One month after the coup, the secondary school division of the ministry issued new guidelines for the teaching of history, including an instructive that "the industrial revolution should be treated, as its name indicates, in terms of changes in science and technology, eliminating the theories and conflicts attending political and social discussions that are now sufficiently well known" (*El Mercurio*, October 18, 1973). A circular of the Command of the Military Institutes required all school principals in Santiago to channel "all matters [pertaining to] the security of their schools or administrative and teaching elements that constitute problems" to the military authorities. The junta ordered the denunciation of all "irregularities" related to teachers, students, and parent associations (*centros de padres*), such as "the spreading of jokes or stories about the activities of the Junta or its members, the distortion of patriotic values and concepts" (Comando de Institutos Militares, 1974).

In November 1973, the junta created a commission, with representation of the main association of private Catholic schools, the Federación de Institutos de Educación (FIDE), whose charge was to "revise all elements of the curriculum arbitrarily manipulated by the Marxist government and to evaluate the educational reform process since 1965" (Decreto 1892 de Educación, November 21, 1973). The military authorities also prohibited the application of surveys to schools, developed explicit lists of permissible textbooks and teaching materials, and carefully guarded the entrances to many educational establishments (Núñez 1984). The regime instituted programs to promote patriotic values on a weekly basis in all schools, and added several weeklong units to the elementary school curriculum in 1974: one coinciding with the date of the coup and focusing on the army, a week on naval victories, another on the heroes of Concepción, Bernardo O'Higgins week, and a week on the national founders (Ministerio de Educación 1974). The inspection of schools by the commanders of the military institutes of Santiago continued until the beginning of the municipalization process in 1979.

The ferocity of the junta's ideological warfare was the result and extension of the highly polarized, fierce communist and anticommunist rhetoric that had surrounded the Allende government. Led by a group of ardent socialists in the Ministry of Education, particularly Superintendent Iván Núñez, the Unidad Popular government sought to consolidate and unify the variety of Chilean educational establishments into one centralized organization, the Escuela Nacional Unificada (ENU), that would create a "New Man" beyond "bourgeois domination" and would emphasize vocational training and labor. The more radical members of the ruling coalition referred on occasion to the coming elimination of private schooling in Chile (Farrell 1986, 77). This would have been a highly charged statement in any Chilean government, given the history of political battles between Liberals and Conservatives over the liberties of private, Catholic education; but it was explosive coming from an allegedly anti-Catholic, communistic regime. The elimination of private schools would violate not only the constitutional right to educational freedom, *la libertad de enseñanza,* but one of the five components of the 1970 "Statute of Guarantees," a document of Allende's promises given in exchange for Christian Democratic support. As a result, the oppo-

Teachers march during a strike in Santiago, 1993. Courtesy of the Chilean Embassy.

sition vilified the ENU. It is not at all clear that the Allende government intended to eliminate private schools, but the controversy surrounding the ENU served the critical function of uniting the opposition and lending moral justification to a military overthrow.[3]

When the regime would move from its initial phase of repression to consolidation and institutional transformation, beginning sometime around 1978 with the first plebiscite and the enactment of the new labor law, it had no real opposition. The legacy of the communist past, lingering guerrilla attacks from groups like the Movimiento de Izquierdo Revolucionario, and the regime's claim to rule on the basis of national security gained it enough legitimacy with the public to carry through policy reforms. The principal institution whose support the military needed, the Church, at first supported the coup and the regime's policies in education because they opposed the legacy of the ENU. As evidence of widespread repression and torture mounted, however, elements of the Church grew hostile to the regime; and some openly criticized the major educational reforms when the regime sketched them in 1979 and 1980. These criticisms were neither strong nor widely shared enough, however, to derail the regime's reforms. The relative autonomy of the military government made it possible to conceive and initiate neoliberal reforms in the social sectors.

Divisions Among Policy-Making Elites in the Military Regime

Despite its relative autonomy from civil society, the political parties, and the extant governmental bureaucracy, the regime's post-welfare policies in education suffered from all of the contradictions and incoherencies described in chapter 2. The source of most of these inconsistencies lay in the varying motives, different worldviews, and incompatible policy vocabularies of the several groups responsible for the reforms. The larger causes were rapidly changing domestic priorities and Pinochet's frequent and unexpected shifts in civilian personnel, a typically authoritarian pattern designed to undercut potential rivals. Nine different education ministers served the junta from 1979 to 1990. These shifts, in turn, illustrated the regime's relative indifference to municipal education as such.[4] What was important was that public education and the rhetoric around it be consonant with the ideological principles of *subsidiariedad* and *libertad de enseñanza,* and for it not to hinder the macroeconomic balance and short-term growth. Teacher strikes and municipal deficits were also important educational issues for the junta because they were highly visible. Actual and demonstrable improvement in the quality of subsidized education was not a critical goal because, as was the case in prior Chilean governments, most of the influential individuals and interest groups in Chile sent their children to private paid schools—there remained little political pressure to improve subsidized education.

Essentially four distinct groups controlled decision making in educational policy between 1979 and the arrival of the democratic government: Minister of Education Gonzalo Vial, who wrote the presidential directive of 1979 and under whose leadership the reform plans initially took shape; three officials in the neoliberal mold, Juan Carlos Méndez, Miguel Kast, and Maria Teresa Infante, who designed and implemented the educational modernization; the military officers who ran the Ministry of Interior and who, because mayors reported to them, effectively implemented educational policies; and the civilian ministers from 1985 on, who reactivated the functions of the traditional education bureaucracy. Examining them in turn illustrates the wide discrepancies in their goals and language and helps to explain the contradictions of Chilean educational policy in the military regime.

The first of the principal figures was Gonzalo Vial, minister from December 26, 1978, to December 14, 1979. A member of a leading Chilean family and a major historian, Vial was the first civilian minister of education under the military regime (excepting José Navarro Tobar, who served on an interim basis the first two weeks after the 1973 coup). That Pinochet would bring in a notable civilian with an independent source of authority suggests both that Pinochet perceived his hold on power to be firm and that an effort to transform and not merely repress social forces was under way.

Vial's thinking on the education reforms was consistent with the military regime's approach, which sought a marriage of neoliberal and anticommunist principles. In the Conservative tradition of *la libertad de enseñanza,* Vial wanted to return schools to the control of communities and families. He wrote Pinochet's 1979 Presidential Directive on education, which was the first communication from the regime that carried the weight and publicity of a major policy statement on education. Although it made no reference to the transfer of schools to municipalities or to an attendance-based funding mechanism, it described steps taken to deconcentrate the ministry, which it conceived as a long and gradual process bringing decision making closer to students and parents and whose ultimate goal was family control of schools: privatization. The organisms of private control were sketchy, but it contemplated "Provincial Services of Public Education," new autonomous community-based bodies, initially merely consultative but that would eventually have decision-making power, whose task would be to "supervise" the ministry's regional secretariats (SEREMIs).[5] The document contains an interesting, new conceptualization of an education ministry whose main tasks are supervisory and normative, not administrative; but it also demonstrates the vagueness of the regime's formulations just a year and a half before municipalization.

Vial wanted the regime to spend much more on education than it did and advocated funding levels more than three times greater than those eventually adopted in the subvention scheme. He also forwarded a plan to create libraries in all Chilean schools (the great majority lack them), a proposal that the Ministry of Finance rejected for budgetary reasons (Cox 1985). Protesting the regime's human rights violations, Vial resigned from the cabinet on December 14, 1979. The power to plan for and design the educational modernization then moved entirely to the DIRPRES (Budget Office) in the Ministry of Finance.[6] With Vial's departure, the pedagogical elements of educational modernization began to receive less attention than those relating to incentives and to the post-welfare vision; and real community control of schools, though a purported goal of the reforms, lost their strongest advocate.

The planning and design for educational modernization then fell to the budget chief in the DIRPRES, Juan Carlos Méndez, and to the ODEPLAN (National Planning Office) director, Miguel Kast; and responsibility for its implementation fell largely to the superintendent of education, María Teresa Infante. All three were economists of the Chicago mold. The three main elements of the educational reform, the application of the private labor code to teachers, the transfer of schools to the municipalities, and the creation of the subvention mechanism, took shape under their leadership.

They believed that eliminating civil service rigidities in education was critical. According to theory, service delivery with labor markets was much more efficient than public sector organization; and in the case of Chile, teachers' strikes throughout history had seriously damaged education and polarized sectoral politics. Ending them once and for all, which the combination of applying the private sector labor code to teachers and transferring school ownership to municipalities would accomplish, could liberate service delivery from politics and rent-seeking. (It would also, of course, weaken the labor movement and any future socialist and communist parties, a result that served the regime's ideological goals.) Infante described their position:

> The administrative is in the service of the technical. Maybe I have not explained this well. I believe that there existed an objective of elevating the level and restoring the value of the properly technical-educative, that had been absolutely lost, having been put in the service of the administrative. Because the administrative was what was urgent: any government would fall the day that salaries were not paid on time, and, well, with fifteen hundred public employees paying the salaries by hand, God help us, this could happen any day! (Cox 1985, 163)

For the neoliberals, the purpose of the second element of the reform, municipalization, was not, as it was for Vial, to bring families into educational decision making. Rather, it was seen as a prescription for efficiency taken from the theory of public choice. Government would be more efficient, the neoliberals believed, if localities possessed broader discretion to spend and to tax. In what now seems like eminent intellectual fuzziness, however, they advocated municipalization knowing full well the constraints on local finance that existed and that were likely to remain. Infante believed that the "closeness of municipalities to the world of [educational] establishments favors more agile decision making and a better allocation of resources"

(Cox 1985, 109). The meaning of "closeness," as well as the political and economic signals associated with municipalization, were not analyzed in detail. An internal DIRPRES document argued for broad participation of families and communities in educational decision making, but the regime preferred to transfer schools to alcaldes alone because of the need for univocal authority.[7]

The third element of the reforms, the subvention mechanism, allocated state educational resources to consumers to utilize as they chose. Taken from the emphasis on "subsidies to demand" in the 1972 neoliberal manifesto *El Ladrillo*, the subventions were to operate like Milton Friedman's vouchers, promoting public-private competition in the system (*"El Ladrillo"* 1992). The public justification for the subvention, however, almost never centered on competition or on problems with public sector property rights, as Friedman or another Chicago economist might have described those terms. (Indeed, the word *competition* almost never appeared in the regime documents of the period.) Although Méndez believed that the term was widely used, Infante conceded that they avoided the word because it made teachers and others anxious (interview, May 27, 1994). Rather, the subvention created an "even playing field" between public and private schools, a conception of the public and the secular dating back to the nineteenth-century battles between Liberals and Conservatives over the Church's educational authority.

For instance, when Minister of Education Alfredo Prieto (December 14, 1979, to April 4, 1982) used the term *competition,* which was not very often, he needed to suggest that its destructive elements could be ameliorated. In his book describing the new system of education, he suggests that modernization leads to competition between private schools and municipal councils of community development (consisting of alcaldes, their advisors, and unspecified community representatives) on the basis of quality improvements. (Competition on the basis of attracting better endowed students is not considered.) He contends that "the new system's design permits higher wages to be paid to the best teachers," and that the "community, which is represented by the council of community development, will protect its good teachers, given its interest in its own progress and in that of its children." What signals would lead municipal governments to care about local education, and how teachers will be evaluated by school owners and municipal councils, are not discussed. Prieto also asserts that if quality were to decline in a school, a parent could then alertly enroll his child in a better one "without it costing him any more." But what then would happen to the abandoned, low-quality school? Prieto, like most of his counterparts, refuses to address school closures: "most likely in this case, the community, through its council of communal development, will take the necessary measures to remedy the situation that is affecting the quality of education" (Prieto 1983, 84–85, 93–94).

A third account of the goals of the education reforms emerges in the speeches of military officers. It is important to remember that they occupied a great number of posts in regional and local government, including many of the mayoralties, and that all alcaldes were subordinated to the Ministry of the Interior. The military government implemented the post-welfare incentive structures on the ground; and whatever the planners might or might not have said about competition, participation, and choice, at the local level control and hierarchy were probably more important than ever. Although few accounts of local educational decision making under the military regime exist, a speech from Subsecretary of Interior Enrique Montero, a career air force officer, in a Ministry of Finance handbook on the reforms sheds light on the way military officials understood them:

> This new institutional structure aims at, first, an administrative decentralization which gives more flexibility and efficiency to municipal promotion of the community's real needs; second, greater autonomy and freedom for the activities of the Alcalde which permit him to discover sufficiently well the wishes of the local community for the sake of an appropriate application of the principle of *subsidiariedad* and of the right participation of intermediary organizations of the community; and third, an increase in financial resources that ought to translate into a display of community integration and progress. (Montero 1980, 19)

Note that the municipality promotes the community's "real" needs; that the Alcalde, not the community, is "autonomous"; he discovers the wishes of the community "sufficiently" well; *subsidiariedad* is applied "appropriately"; the community is involved in "right" participation; and that progress is related to communal "integration." Elsewhere in the speech Montero explains that the mechanism for improving school quality is the petitioning of unelected military officials by ordinary Chileans: "the community will be personally interested in a school that belongs to it, will require of the alcalde an outlay from the municipal budget." In places Montero's speech sounds like a nineteenth-century relic, with language reminiscent of the glory days of the Chilean Radical Party: "The value of extending the world of education is undoubted . . . especially when those who are sunk in ignorance notice just how important is the emancipation from such slavery." That language of liberation, borrowed from the enlightenment liberals of the nineteenth century and here applied to the historic mission of the military, would seem to justify a strong central government role in education (Montero 1980, 24–25). It is not surprising, then, that most of the criticisms of educational modernization emphasize that the decentralization of authority did anything but promote responsiveness and flexibility in schools (Magendzo 1988; Schiefelbein and Apablaza 1984).

Fourth, after 1984 or 1985, when Pinochet endorsed the policies of an economic team focusing on a more "pragmatic" form of neoliberalism, the Ministry of Education assumed a more active role in policy making. Particularly under René Salamé, who served as minister from April 28, 1989, to March 10, 1990, but who had also been an influential subsecretary during the preceding years, the career bureaucrats in the Ministry of Education started to issue more decrees regulating the infrastructure and operations of private schools, limiting competition in certain areas, and determining personnel policies in the municipalities. This change in the regime's stance was partly a consequence of Salamé's initiative—he was an educator and not a neoliberal by training—but it was also tied to the coming plebiscite (interview with René Salamé, July 19, 1994). By 1985, the regular and widespread strikes and protests of the early 1980s had subsided, the paramilitary threats to the regime were mostly eliminated, and the state of the economy had improved. The political opposition would soon recognize that its best chance at ending military rule was to accept the Constitution of 1980 and to campaign against Pinochet in the plebiscite of 1988. The regime, confident of its achievements and seeking to legitimize its status with a popular mandate, began to tolerate dissent and some political mobilization. In education, this meant that the Colegio de Profesores was permitted to elect its own leader in 1985 and that educators who had been clandestinely criticizing the regime's neoliberal policies came public. The impact of these events at the municipal level was that both military and civilian alcaldes, anticipating the need for either their own or the regime's electoral support, began to seek the favor of now mobilizing teachers. They sought central government coverage of their education "deficits" because they did not want the responsibility for laying off teachers or running shoddy schools. The ministry bureaucrats, themselves mostly teachers, as well as many of the alcaldes, together sought to mitigate the effect of the post-welfare incentive system as best they could. As a result, the ministry issued rules and regulations inconsistent with post-welfare incentives that took shape in the latter years of the military regime.

These divisions among policy-making elites in the military regime had a number of consequences for the post-welfare incentive structures. First, central government regulations remained in effect, and in some ways grew stronger, during a process of decentralization and privatization. Second, the incentives of teachers fundamentally did not change. Although many teachers were dismissed, neither the central government, nor by any means the municipalities, attempted to create a system tying performance to wages and advancement. In fact, the military government adopted some measures directly opposed to making incentives work properly, such as municipal deficit coverage. Third, the educational system suffered from underfinancing because no single voice articulated the need for more funds. And finally, no agent could overcome the military's aversion to authentic community participation; and the failure of the regime to develop the infrastructure necessary for competition, such as its inability to generate public acceptance for a widely disseminated independent standardized test, made the parental exercise of informed choice impossible.

Despite the autonomy the military regime enjoyed, Méndez, Kast, Infante, de Castro, and the other "Chicago boys" could not transform educational worldviews by themselves, which was necessary for the reforms to take root. Autonomy from interest groups gave the planners the capacity to issue the reform decrees, but they also needed to change the educational beliefs of those Chileans without direct material interests in the old system, such as government officials, military leaders, and the alcaldes. The secrecy and isolation associated with their powers prevented the wide public debate necessary to change basic education.

Contradictions and Policy Reversals in the Democratic Government

The prospects for the post-welfare reforms in education seemed ambiguous when the Aylwin administration assumed power on March 11, 1990. On the one hand, the teachers' unions, angry at widespread and apparently arbitrary dismissals during the military government and resentful at the decline in their real wages and their loss of prestige, were demanding job stability, a law granting them professional status, and substantial salary increases. They had borne the costs of economic adjustment as much as any other group during the 1980s, and the Chilean political tradition of *reivindicaciones,* in which interest groups who make sacrifices or are forgotten in

Augusto Pinochet shakes hands with Patricio Aylwin during the transfer of power, San tiago, 1990. Courtesy of the Chilean Embassy.

one period are entitled to redress (Valenzuela 1978), indicated that they wer due. They had campaigned against Pinochet in the plebiscite and had clos ties to the leaders of the Concertación parties, who generally supported pro grams to restore dignity and stability to teachers. The "programa" of th Concertación, for example, argued that "the full recognition of the dignit of teaching, as well as the support and respect of the society for the optima fulfillment of its important tasks, are necessary factors for the improvemen of the quality of education." For that end, it advocated "an improvement i the salaries of teachers, . . . greater stability, the end of the arbitrary cessatio of functions." It was also critical of what it called "alcaldización" and "abuse in the administration of municipal schools" (Concertación 1989, 23–24).

Both the teachers and the political parties emphasized job stability i large part for political reasons: the great majority of alcaldes were Pinoche appointees who would remain in office until the municipal elections of Jun 1992, and whose powers over the hiring and firing of school personne insulted and demoralized the teachers. One story among many described how the alcalde of Antofogasta paid a first-year teacher what teachers with thirty years of experience normally earn simply because she was the daughter of the Appeals Court in that city.[8] The importance of job stability, however, whatever its political overtones, also threatened to dismantle one of the essential elements of the neoliberal modernization: the use of private sector labor markets to allocate teaching according to families' choices.

On the other hand, the coalition that assumed power in March 1990, though it included a nominally socialist party, was friendly toward the private sector; and it endorsed decentralization, efficiency in government, and privatization where necessary. Its program for government recognized the principle of *la libertad de enseñanza* (with the implicit acknowledgment of the rights of children in private school to equivalent subventions), called administrative decentralization in education "a basic and fundamental principle," supported private sector involvement in education, and advocated the democratization of the municipal and regional frameworks as the best means to improve public education (Concertación 1989, 23–24). Several government leaders had spent their exile in Western Europe, where they grew to believe in the importance of private property rights, capitalism, and a sound macroeconomy, as well as in the compatibility of those goals with progressivism and a concern for equality (Cuevas 1993; Walker 1990). Though critical of the equity effects of neoliberalism, the Christian Democratic politicians who led the governing coalition clearly supported private sector initiatives, centrist macroeconomic policies, and government efficiency. As a result, it was also possible that the government might choose to retain and enrich the educational modernization of 1981 with salary adjustments, the professionalization of teaching, and municipal democratization.

Even if it had wanted, the Aylwin government arguably did not possess the constitutional power to reverse the transfer of schools to municipalities, nor perhaps to rescind the system of equal per-pupil financing for the municipal and private subsidized sectors. On March 10, 1990, the day before leaving power, the military regime had passed the Constitutional Organic Law of Education (Ley 18.926, the "LOCE"), which the Constitution of 1980 had called for but which the regime had taken ten years to draft, refine, and adopt. It stipulated that it is both the duty and the "preferential right" of parents to educate children, a clause that many interpreted as establishing a constitutional foundation for municipal control of education and for the subvention mechanism.[9] The Concertación did not possess the votes in the Senate to amend the constitutional organic law because of the presence of eight unelected or "institutional senators," a legacy of Pinochet's Constitution of 1980, and because of binomial, list-based electoral rules that overrepresented the minority parties. Even if the LOCE did not in fact provide a foundation for the post-welfare reforms, many believed that it did; and reversing them would have required a sustained and difficult political fight with the opposition that the Concertación would not want to risk.

In its first major actions and speeches in social policy, the Aylwin government quickly reiterated its desire to redress the decline in health and education spending during the 1980s. In a speech shortly after taking office, Aylwin reaffirmed his desire to focus on social policy (*El Mercurio*, March 14, 1990). The Colegio de Profesores was the first group to receive an official invitation to the presidential palace (*Historia de Ley* 1992, 2277). The government then pushed for and achieved, with the votes of the major opposition party, Renovación Nacional, an increase in the value added tax to finance additional expenditures in health and education over the next three years. Expenditures in the social sectors would then increase by over 30 percent during the Aylwin government, and members of the administration would credit those expenditures (as well as the high rate of economic growth) for the drop in absolute poverty in the country from 40 percent in 1989 to 28 percent in 1994, according to official figures (Larrañaga 1994).

The presidency sent a comprehensive education sector proposal to the Congress on October 16, 1990. It would focus the revenues from the tax reform on several areas (including an adjustment in teachers' salaries), grant teachers a degree of job stability, and recognize that teachers were not ordinary private sector workers by establishing a body of law specifically to govern their profession. Teachers had long sought a special piece of legislation that recognized the uniqueness of their practice, and officials in the military regime had attempted to draw up a draft Estatuto Docente, or "Teachers' Law," for the education sector; but the teachers had found this law insufficient. The Estatuto Docente from the Concertación did satisfy most of the teachers' essential demands. It would raise the national minimum for teacher salaries in both municipal and private subsidized schools, establish a graduated pay scale based on years of experience for teachers in the municipal sector, create a fund to pay for teachers' continuing education, require public competition for the filling of all posts in the education sector, establish the mechanism by which the number of teaching posts in each municipality would be set jointly by the municipal administrations and the Ministry of Education, and limit the reasons for which teachers in municipal schools could be dismissed or transferred. The teachers had sought a higher minimum salary, but the union settled for the final version of the legislation with the understanding that salaries would gradually be increased over the next several years. Although the legislation took much longer than the executive had anticipated to get through Congress, its final form received unanimous approval in the Congress on June 27, 1991 (*Historia de Ley* 1992).

The adoption of the Estatuto Docente, though not recentralizing public education under the central ministry and not rescinding the subvention mechanism, constituted a clear departure from the post-welfare model as Kast, Méndez, and Infante had conceived it. Supply rigidities would limit the response of the market to parents' choices. The creation of special, extra-subventional funds to pay for the salary minimums and other payments to teachers would undo the strict tie between municipal schools' revenues and their ability to attract students. At the same time, however, the Estatuto endorsed the municipalization of education, and it granted powers to munic-ipalities that, although supposedly already theirs under the military regime, were effectively controlled or influenced centrally under the authoritarian hierarchies, such as setting the size of municipal teaching staffs.[10] It also cod-ified certain contradictions inherited from the previous government, such as the continuing distinction between the technical-pedagogical and the administrative: although municipalities would eventually become politically (and soon electorally) accountable for the quality of education, the ministry retained the responsibility to assess and to guarantee school performance, teacher training, and curricula.

Succeeding events suggested a policy reversal: it seemed that the demo-cratic government wanted, despite the Estatuto Docente, to move toward marketlike incentives in basic education. First, during Senate debate over an extension of the tax reforms in 1993, which were essential to the social sec-tor policy of the Concertación, members of the opposition party, the RN, exacted government approval of a system called *financiamiento compartido,* or "shared financing," in exchange for voting to renew the value-added taxes. The system would permit municipal high schools and all private subsidized schools to levy "voluntary" fees on all students as a means of raising educa-tion revenues. Minister of Finance Alejandro Foxley first agreed, then struck the provision, but finally embraced it (Actas de Discusión Senado Sesión 23a, September 8, 1993; Actas de Discusión Cámara Sesión 26a, August 10, 1993). The teachers' union, as well as the former minister of education and political leader, Ricardo Lagos, viewed the government concession as an attack on Chile's tradition of public education and as an endorsement of neoliberal policies in the sector (*El Mercurio*, September 11, 1993).

Second, the government launched an effort to retract elements of the Estatuto Docente. A ministry study found that although municipal enrollments increased only 2.9 percent between 1991 and 1994, teaching hours rose by 5.9 percent, and teaching personnel under contract by 9.6 percent. It also confirmed the widely known discrepancy between the student-teacher ratios (which include administrators) in the private subsidized sector, around 45 students to one teacher, and the municipal sector, about 21 students per teacher (Division de Planificación y Presupesto 1994). The impossibility of relocating teachers from one municipality to another or even from one school to another without a teacher's consent, a legacy of the Estatuto Docente, was a major contributing factor in the municipal deficits: schools could not adjust their staffing levels when enrollments changed. Several officials in the ministries of education, finance, and interior believed that there were too many teachers in the municipal sector, and one official, Subsecretary of Regional Development (SUBDERE) Jorge Rodríguez Grossi, created a controversy when he stated that view publicly (*El Mercurio*, April 20, 1994).

The necessary amendments to the Estatuto Docente were postponed until after the elections of September 1993. In a political miscalculation, the new Concertación government of President Eduardo Frei Ruiz-Tagle quickly followed through on the plans of the previous administration, proposing amendments to the Estatuto Docente that would permit the transfer or even the dismissal of teachers following enrollment declines. The leadership of the Colegio de Profesores was outraged not only at the amendments themselves but at the fact it had not been consulted before the legislation was sent to the Congress. A work stoppage followed on May 17, 1994; and the threat of an indefinite strike loomed if the government did not withdraw the legislation. Negotiations between the Colegio and the government did avert a national strike, but they did not settle the basic disagreement. The two sides grew further apart, and in August 1994, following a near breakdown in negotiations, Frei was forced to replace his education minister, the independent economist Ernesto Schiefelbein, with the Christian Democrat and seasoned political figure, Sergio Molina. After months of negotiation Molina did manage to reach a compromise with the teachers' union and gain congressional approval of the amendments to the Estatuto Docente in September 1995 (Ley 19.410). The amendments permitted municipalities to reduce their teaching staffs according to Annual Plans for the Development of Municipal Education (PADEMs), but to date very few teachers have been dismissed. The antagonistic relations between the teachers and the executive seemed likely to continue in light of the election, shortly after the compromise, of the Communist Jorge Pávez to the presidency of the Colegio de Profesores.

Third, in September 1995 a high-level commission on education appointed by Frei, recognizing the effect of the Estatuto Docente on teachers' performance incentives, called the results of that legislation "catastrophic." It called for merit pay, hiring flexibility at the school level, and the transfer of subvention revenues directly to schools so that the high-performing establishments in a municipality would stop subsidizing those that were performing poorly. With that report, improving the post-welfare incentives again became a policy goal of the Concertación government.[11]

The Political Sources of the Democratic Regime's Education Policies

What factors explain the educational policy reversals and contradictions in the Concertación government? This account focuses on four explanatory factors: the ambiguity of the regime's ideological commitment and its effect on the institutional setting, the influence of teachers on both the government and the opposition, the growing disenchantment with the union leaders on the part of the rank and file, and changes in political leadership of the democratic government.

The regime's ideological commitment to post-welfare incentive structures was ambiguous from the beginning. Although it endorsed two key elements of the 1980 modernization, the municipal control of schools and the subvention mechanism, its rhetoric usually portrayed municipalization as a means to promote civil society and local democracy. Only rarely did the government justify it in the language of public choice theory. Similarly, endorsements of the subvention mechanism usually concerned a "level playing field" or the tradition of *la libertad de enseñanza,* which arguably requires equal treatment of secular and parochial schools. The words *competition* and *incentives* rarely appear, if at all, in the speeches of the government's education ministers, in the party platforms, and in speeches on the Congress floor.[12] The ambiguity was obvious in the "programa" of the Concertación, which praised decentralization at the same time that it supported the "unity" of the national system (Concertación 1989, 21).

Paradoxically, although its ideology supported decentralization and privatization, the Concertación first sought a national and uniform remedy for educational problems. Its actions created an expectation, both in the government and among teachers and the society at large, that educational problems would be negotiated and solved at the national level again in the future. Moreover, the remedy offered, the Estatuto Docente, established financial and statutory arrangements in which the central government, not the municipalities, negotiated with the Colegio de Profesores for wages and working conditions. Teachers learned to take grievances to the Ministries of Education and Finance and not to municipalities and private school owners. Meanwhile, the government's ideology committed it to extend increasing powers over curriculum, personnel, and school governance to the localities. The teachers' union was playing the old game whose rules derived from the *estado docente,* in which it could win concessions by pressuring the central ministries, while the central government wanted to believe that it no longer possessed the keys to educational decision making. The two sides misunderstood the rules the other was using, and negotiations eventually broke down.

The lack of clarity in the government's purposes, which had been partly a strategic ambiguity to appeal to different constituencies, partly an example of the ideological challenges facing the Left and Center-Left, and partly mere confusion and inexperience,[13] allowed for an institutional framework in which teachers' interests mobilized nationally at the same time that the government's capacity to handle those demands was continuing to be decentralized. Had the democratic government's objectives in education been clearer at that euphoric moment of transition when it both enjoyed a degree of autonomy from organized interest groups and possessed unique political strength (managing the tax increase for social expenditures, for instance), it might have established a policy regime that prevented or at least limited the mobilization of interests at the national level. Interest group pressures, changing political leaders, and party dynamics all affected the course of educational policy making under the regime; but the relationships among those variables were dynamic. The institutional framework of the Estatuto Docente shaped the ways in which they could interact, exacerbating the tensions likely to develop in a pluralist, democratic regime.[14]

The most striking aspect of the impact of teachers' interests on educational policy was their influence on the opposition. One would have thought that the Concertación alone would have ears for their grievances and wishes. After all, most of the union leaders are members of the Concertación parties;[15] the opposition parties continue to support the educational policies of the military regime, which the great majority of teachers resent; and neither the RN nor the UDI count teachers or unions among its base constituency. Nevertheless, the deliberations regarding the Estatuto Docente made it evident that teachers' interests were affecting the votes and speeches of politicians on the Right. For instance, several opposition speeches on the Senate and House floors berated the government for raising teacher salaries so little. Some accused the Ministry of Education and other government bodies of only listening to the leaders of the Colegio de Profesores, not to the rank and file, and boasted of the meetings they had with teachers in their districts. Others listed the various amendments to the government bill that they had sponsored on behalf of the Colegio, such as lowering the permissible class size from forty-five to thirty-five, compensating rural teachers at higher rates, including kindergarten teachers in the reach of the Estatuto Docente, and permitting teachers to receive eleven months of severance pay in the event of dismissal (in place of the bill's six months). Some sought to increase teachers' salaries by more than the bill allowed, while other opposition congressmen pushed to remove the clause that would permit teachers to be dismissed in the event that student enrollments fell in a municipality.[16] The influence of the teachers' union on the opposition was also visible during the strikes and negotiations surrounding the Frei government's attempt in April 1994 to reinstate the clause permitting teachers to be transferred or dismissed if enrollments fell: in addition to opposition from Concertación legislators, the proposal drew criticism from several congressmen on the Right, who expressed their concerns publicly and vocally (*La Epoca*, May 3, 1994; *El Mercurio*, May 15, 1994).

Understanding the reasons for the influence of teachers on the Right requires an account of the structure of local politics in Chile. Whereas Chilean politics at the central level is known for its highly ideological character, municipal-level politics before the 1973 coup was highly particularized. Traditionally, it involved a great deal of "brokerage" transactions between local officials and Santiago-based national politicians: local councilmen and mayors rounded up electoral support for congressmen, who then in turn brokered constituent services and budgetary outlays for their local districts, their constituents, and for the mayors and councilmen who helped them. Analyzing Chilean politics in the 1960s, Valenzuela described the relationship in detail: "A candidate for Congress sought commitments from local people of influence who could mobilize their own supporters in his behalf. As one popular *regidor* put it, 'We are the work tools of the *parlamentarios*'" (Valenzuela 1977, 131). Although the political institutions of Chile remained nascent in 1990, these relationships between congressmen (*diputados*) and local brokers held firm. The UDI in particular drew many of its political leaders and candidates from former alcaldes appointed under Pinochet, and its *diputados* had a stake in maintaining and cultivating relationships with local municipal officials with whom they had worked.

Teachers in Chile were traditionally among the most important local leaders in their communities, particularly in rural areas, where they often enjoyed respect for being among the only professionals in their districts; and *diputados* were forced to rely on them to organize local opinions and votes. With the return of electoral politics to Chile in 1988, and the advent of municipal elections in 1992, teachers institutionalized their social positions at the local level by running for and gaining office as community councilmen (*concejales*). Data from the electoral commission, in table 7, show that "teacher" was the most common occupation among *concejales* in the nation, and that among the occupations requiring a university education, teachers were almost six times as numerous as the other professions. The part-time nature of the position of *concejal*, as well as the relatively low pay *concejales* received for their work, makes the position attractive to teachers but not to other professionals such as lawyers or doctors. As a result, *diputados* and *senadores* from all parties sought to gain the favor of the teachers in their districts.

Table 7. Most Common Occupations of Municipal Council Members in Chile, 1994 (in percent)

Teachers	17
Farmers, cultivators, seasonal agricultural workers	16
Shopkeepers, local vendors	12
Clerks, janitors, office workers	12
Accountants	3
Lawyers	3
Doctors	3
Skilled workers	3
Factory workers	3
Students	2
Drivers	1
Architects	1
Business executives	1

Source: Tabulated from Servicio Electoral, República de Chile, 1994.
Note: Percentages are rounded to the nearest whole number. There were 2,082 municipal council members in the registry. The category "retired," though one of the most common responses, is excluded.

Although gaining teacher support at the national level, from the directorate of the Colegio de Profesores, required an ideological shift not possible for parties on the Right, given their social bases and party platforms and the strong historical and personal ties between national teacher leaders and the Concertación, opposition politicians could build loyalties at the level of their individual districts by championing the bread-and-butter issues for teachers in the early 1990s: job stability and pay. And given the ideological ambiguities in the educational policies of both the Concertación and the military regime in its latter years, they could do this with relatively little cost to their parties' positions. Members of the RN and the UDI distinguished between supporting the directorate of the Colegio de Profesores, which the Concertación did and whom they accused of being elitist (in the tradition of Rightist populist nationalism), and supporting the base of teachers in Chile, which they claimed to do. In the process, they discovered an interest in making the Estatuto Docente even more favorable to teachers than it was originally, which led to an excessively rigid employment stability for teachers, and which then forced the government to seek to modify the legislation just one year later.

Increasing militancy and divisions in the teachers' union also affected Concertación educational policies. There were signs of mounting disenchantment in the union even during the negotiations surrounding the Estatuto Docente, but expressions of disagreement became evident after the law's passage. The leadership had originally demanded a national minimum salary of 150 thousand pesos per month, with an experience-based graduated pay scale built on that figure; but after the government argued that it could not go that high, it settled for a gradual increase to a minimum salary of 100 thousand pesos per month. Most teachers were disappointed, and the union leadership was compelled to announce national strikes when in both 1992 and 1993 the government continued to resist its salary demands. During the 1993 protests, regional branches of the Colegio de Profesores marched out on several "wildcat" strikes even after the national directorate had settled into negotiations with the government. In the regions around Antofogasta, the Bio-Bio, Aysen, and Magallanes, some of the wildcat strikes lasted for weeks and months; and local union leaders called for the resignation of President Verdugo (*El Siglo*, September 6, 1993; *El Mercurio*, September 5, 18, 1993).

The cause of the internal union divisions was a growing perception among union members that the directorate was placing its own political interests before those of the union base. Often in Chile, the leadership of union organizations has served as a stepping-stone to national politics or to a post in the ministry. The former vice-president of the Colegio, Julio Val-ladares, for example, moved to occupy the position of subsecretary of educa-tion in 1992; and, surprisingly for the union, his negotiating position with his excolleagues seemed especially harsh. In addition, three other union lead-ers, including the president of the Colegio, Osvaldo Verdugo (PDC), ran as candidates for the Cámara in the internal party nominations. Rank-and-file teachers believed that Verdugo and the others were refusing to take a hard-line stance with the government in order not to alienate their party leaders in the government. This would become clear in the 1995 elections for the presidency of the Colegio, when the teachers gave Jorge Pávez, a Communist and an advocate of a tougher bargaining posture with the government, the plurality of votes. As a result of the growing militancy of the teachers and the increasing pressure on their leaders to make stronger demands on the gov-ernment, the capacity of the parties to manage teachers' wage demands weak-ened; and the possibility of forging a consensus around the post-welfare incentive structures grew more remote.

Finally, Concertación educational policy also reflected changes in polit-ical leadership. For the first minister of education, Ricardo Lagos, a noted PPD leader with presidential ambitions, making a mark on educational pol-icy, particularly one to benefit a potentially influential constituency, was an important political goal. The Estatuto Docente represented enough of an attack on neoliberalism to match his ideological position, and it gained suf-ficient support from the teachers to create sympathy and obligations on his behalf (though he recognized that a large number of teachers would have preferred renewed centralization and promised, perhaps disingenuously, to take up that issue at another time).[17] The two ministers who followed Lagos, Jorge Arrate and Ernesto Schiefelbein, did not have similar political ambi-tions and could afford more direct confrontations with the teachers' unions. At the same time, high-level decisions to target other competing needs and a drop in government revenues as a result of a decline in copper prices and the Central Bank's adjustment program of 1990 limited the availability of funds for further increases in teacher salaries. That reality in turn would lead a powerful figure, former finance minister Alejandro Foxley, to decline the education portfolio in 1994. Although Lagos accepted an appointment to lead the Ministry of Public Works, Foxley declined education because he (reportedly) did not believe the position matched his stature, because he pre-ferred the presidency of the PDC in order to position himself for the presi-dential elections (he in fact did assume leadership of the party in 1994), and because the options facing the education minister would unavoidably lead him to take controversial and politically damaging positions. Frei later managed to raise the profile of education by appointing an extraministerial, high-level commission to explore the area and by then selecting the chair of that commission, José Joaquin Brunner, to serve as his general secretary. Direct presidential attention increases the likelihood that the commission's policy recommendations, some of them quite neoliberal, will be adopted in the future.

Conclusions

The education reforms under Chile's military regime suggest that repressive strategies can shield authoritarian governments from interest group pressures that oppose the implementation of post-welfare social sector reforms. Those governments can redesign school finance, limit union strength, change the juridical status of service providers, and deconcentrate or decentralize service delivery. But because education, and probably health care as well, embraces so many providers and clients, and because it entails highly decentralized and ritualized interactions, changes in the sector, particularly those that touch so directly upon the behavior and attitudes of teachers, occur very slowly and require the support, or at least the acquiescence, of the teachers themselves. Authoritarian regimes are unlikely to gain the support of teachers if they vilify and attack educational unions. The isolation and secrecy characteristic of them, as well as the pattern in which loci of power in those regimes are continually shifting, make it hard to establish the trust and confidence necessary for reforms that take a great deal of time to design, execute, refine, and consolidate.

The policies regarding neoliberalism in basic education in the Chilean democratic regime illustrate the problems for post-welfare reforms under pluralist politics in developing countries. In countries with a strong tradition of centralized education, teachers will be influential figures in rural or marginal areas. That influence will make them particularly important constituents for politicians in the national legislature, and that will pose a serious obstacle to implementing post-welfare reforms. The political strength of the teachers in pluralist systems will depend, obviously, on the extent of their unionization and barriers they face to collective action; but well-elaborated educational ideologies, a shared sense of professional identity, and traditions of educational centralism, characteristics that are common among a number of developing countries, are likely to establish a climate favorable to unionization. If the executive grants concessions to the teachers' unions in an effort to promote the post-welfare incentive structure in the long run, as the Concertación government did by creating extrasubventional funds for teachers' salaries in the Estatuto Docente while at the same time consolidating municipalization, those might only increase the incentives for teachers to mobilize in the short term, complicating the government's long-term goals.

These thoughts suggest that only relatively nonrepressive governments can succeed in implementing post-welfare reforms in education. That success, however, will probably depend on the political and financial resources used to entice teachers to accept a radically new system. Success also requires the recognition of the specific characteristics of the sector.

Implications for the Debate
on School Choice

In most educational systems, teachers and the state have agreed to an implicit pact: teachers accept relatively low wages, and in exchange the state grants them a high degree of employment stability. That tacit agreement suits most teachers, particularly at the primary level, because many of them have chosen their field not for its salary but for its working conditions, including the autonomy of the classroom, summers off, early working days, and little chance of dismissal. The historical origins of the exchange probably lie in the nineteenth-century imagination that reconciled a view of educational systems as corporations, where teachers are considered to be front-line factory workers receiving low wages, and as shelters or orphanages, in which teachers are protectors and caregivers free from the cruelties of local political bosses and unfettered capitalism (Labarca 1939, Tyack 1974). Although the reasons for its existence have changed over time, that pact itself has remained strong and is now a central element of the identity of teachers and of the expectations and bargaining strategies of their unions. For post-welfare proponents, the pact is precisely the problem. On efficiency grounds, they advocate shifting the risk associated with educational performance from the dif-

fuse political responsibility assigned to public officials to specific market consequences for teachers and schools.

Because the Chilean military regime and the neoliberals implemented
the post-welfare model with so much ideological zeal, their modernization
strategies exposed its essential elements. This case study has analyzed the
Chilean education reforms for the purpose of examining those central characteristics, and several key problems in post-welfare policy design have
emerged.

The use of exit signals alone to enhance the performance of elementary
and secondary schools is, for reasons of both politics and policy, ineffective.
At no point did the Chilean military government dismiss teachers or close
schools in response to parental pressures or exit signals. Letting even a bad
school close carries costs, both for the children who have (perhaps rationally)
not yet chosen to exit, and for the teachers who relocate. That results in a
political problem for the government. That political problem might also
contain a policy concern because the practice of education requires stable
relationships. If, moreover, the post-welfare scheme is really a disingenuous
program for load-shedding and deficit reduction at the central level, or if an
ideological attack against the state and civil servants accompanies the
reforms, teachers' morale will decline. In a sector in which service delivery is
so decentralized and isolated, the attitudes and outlook of the providers is
critical.

A second problem for the post-welfare scheme is that centralization in
education is difficult to reverse. In Chile, the tradition of centralization possessed an inertial quality ingrained in the habits and worldviews of bureaucrats, teachers, and the public that was hard to overcome. The Chilean ministry also discovered that supervising pedagogical content, for which
governments cannot avoid being ultimately responsible, entailed not only
drawing up lesson plans but regulating the organization and functioning of
schools' daily activities. The isolation in which educators work, the difficulty
of specifying the mechanisms and evaluating the results of the learning
process, and the fact that young students cannot themselves evaluate their
education make guaranteeing a general education for all citizens difficult. A
simple contract and a curriculum are not enough because so much depends
on the teachers' performance and interpretation of that curriculum. As concerns, both legitimate and exaggerated, mounted over abuses in private subsidized schools, municipal inefficiencies, and national employment and inflation targets, the Chilean ministries regulated both municipal and private
schools more intensively. They set new infrastructure requirements, began to

scrutinize the use and receipt of subvention revenues, and constrained entry and exit in the education market. Private schools were probably regulated more tightly than at any time in Chilean history, a surpassingly paradoxical outcome for a neoliberal project.

Even if in a post-welfare scheme a state manages to restrain its regulatory impulses, the threat of the loss of that restraint will lead to suboptimal investment and innovation on the part of private or quasi-private providers, which will then increase pressure for government regulation and control. That risk also weakens the incentive for schools to compete on the basis of quality because that is the most costly competitive strategy and because they might recover only a fraction of their investments if and when the state intervenes again. The private subsidized schools in Chile did not take advantage of the discretion that was granted to them partly because they did not believe that the state would ever really entrust them with curricular authority. The likelihood that controls will follow state funds is compounded by the fact that teachers, unlike doctors, are usually unable to carve out a domain of practice free from state interference. The sheer number of people in the occupation, the wide accessibility of pedagogical knowledge, and the inability of teachers to restrict entrance into the field and preside over authentic pedagogical knowledge all make teaching a relatively weak profession (Lortie 1969, Friedson 1986). Although teachers in a large number of countries, including Chile, have shown that they possess the political power to block reforms that undercut their job stability, their power to resist regulation and claim a status as professional experts is usually weak.

The study assessed the concern that a voucher-based incentive system in a sector with imperfect information might lead to competition on the basis of lower costs, not on quality or value added. Data from an original survey of 726 Santiago households found that families of students in private subsidized schools possess significantly more income and human capital than their counterparts in municipal schools. Because data at the level of individual students were not available in Chile, it was not possible to construct a model that would determine whether or not private subsidized schools are indeed more effective than municipal schools, as advocates of vouchers contend; but the finding is consistent with the hypothesis that one reason private subsidized schools outperform municipal schools is that they attract more advantaged students. The survey revealed that about 28 percent of students in the subsidized sector in Santiago took a test to enroll in their present school, a surprising result given that such tests are traditionally unacceptable, strongly discouraged by the ministry, and largely clandestine, and a result consistent with the possibility that schools are competing by attracting better students. The survey also found that parents were relatively uninformed about the quality of schools in their choice sets at both regional and municipal levels. For example, most were unable to name two schools in metropolitan Santiago whose test scores were in the upper third for the region.

A model utilizing the data demonstrated that the "choice" system does in fact reward parents who are informed about school quality. According to the model, the probability of a child attending a school in the upper third for the region increased by over 8 percent if a parent was informed. Similarly, parents who felt entitled to their school choice and who used specific indicators to assess school achievement raised that probability by 10 percent and 9 percent, respectively. These figures suggest that a choice system rewards individuals who are informed and motivated. Although that criterion for the distribution of good schools is more egalitarian than one based exclusively on region of residence, it is unlikely to help children from the most disadvantaged families.

The neoliberals in Chile had hoped to move educational policy making beyond the strikes, patronage, and interest group pressures that had characterized the system over the past half century. Their strategy was to create enclaves immune to political influence, such as the Division of the Budget in the Finance Ministry, from which Chilean education could be restructured without interest group pressures. This vision of politics was characteristic of the Chilean neoliberal project as a whole: the military blamed democratic politics for allowing Communist parties to gain power, and the neoliberal economists believed it inevitably led to state monopolies. The two groups found a joint interest in weakening democratic control over society and markets: government would be "subsidiary" to private parties wherever possible.

Some proposals for educational choice, particularly the Chubb and Moe program, are likewise convinced that the market will solve the shortcomings of democratic politics. But the Chilean experience shows that the mobilization of political interests and the need for deliberation and consensus building are crucial for educational policy, even under an authoritarian regime. The Pinochet government could not overcome the traditions of centralism, nor even resist the influence of teachers. Because classroom instruction is always ritualized and decentralized, reforms will not succeed unless they have the cooperation of large segments of society. How to secure that cooperation is not obvious and will, of course, depend on the political habits and institutions of a given country. In the United States, the political fights over school desegregation suggest that open public debate and popular control were counterproductive because white Americans did not possess the conscience to fight racism (Hochschild 1984). The Chilean reforms show that changing educational systems requires not only deliberation and consensus-building, which authoritarian regimes do not do well, but political leadership and some degree of coercion, that elusive mix of power and willing submission entailed in the idea of legitimate public authority.

Contested elections are not themselves sufficient for generating the political support for broad educational reforms. In Chile the democratic government's early policies were inconsistent. The causes of its contradictions and policy reversals were related to the specific trajectory of the government's actions, to the influence of the teachers' union on the opposition parties, to increasing militancy and divisions in the teachers' union, and to changes in the democratic government's political leadership. In Chile, where political parties are strong and pervasive and the habits of local democracy have never been deep, municipal mayors routinely heed their political superiors more often than their electorate. That reveals a critical problem for post-welfare models, which in some forms promote the decentralization of power so that decisions are made "closer" to the people and electoral preferences more closely resemble purchasing decisions. Post-welfare models of this form encounter the same difficulties as traditional service delivery: neither consumers nor voters demand many of the things that they "need," such as good education, strongly enough. The problem is central not only for policy but for social theory generally. Bracketing the theoretical issue, a helpful policy proposal would be to assess the activities of school systems more regularly and thoroughly—ask students and parents what they like and dislike, and routinely measure employment and higher education placements of former students. That might make schools more responsive to their users, increase the quality of educational debates, and build the legitimacy of effective political and educational leaders (Henig 1994).

Other Post-Welfare Reforms

The first lesson from the world's farthest reaching neoliberal experiment in education ought to be that simply replacing professional and bureaucratic organization with a market, such as a demand-determined voucher mechanism, is likely to fail. The Chilean reforms of the 1980s were not practicable, did not turn education upside down, and did not dramatically improve school performance. The difficulties the Chilean reforms encountered took a distinctive form shaped by Chile's institutional landscape, as is always the case with policy reforms, but those difficulties were not merely contingent. They were intrinsic to the post-welfare prescription. Choice is not a panacea.

Nevertheless, school choice might be a useful tool in school systems where professional incentives and political accountability have decayed. That is the argument of advocates of choice experiments in several cities in the United States, including Milwaukee and Cleveland, where a limited number of poor families receive voucher subsidies worth a few thousand dollars toward tuition fees at the private school of their choosing. The value of those experiments depends critically on the specific circumstances of their implementation. "The meaning of choice proposals can only be understood in the context of specific alterations of institutional structures within specific constraints on organization, money, and information" (Elmore 1990, 297).

Some supporters believe that choice could promote diversity in public school systems and support the positive right of parents to educate children in their own religious traditions. Advocates of charter schools and of "public school choice," which allocates students to public schools according to preferences rather than region of residence, make that case. England now practices public school choice, and Sweden has loosened central authority over public schools and introduced subsidies to private schools for the purpose of creating more variety in a "monochrome" public school system. Religion is important for the choice systems in Australia and the Netherlands, both of which subsidize private schools in order to create an even playing field between parochial and state schools. Both the protection of the cultural rights of its Maori minority and efficiency arguments motivate New Zealand's system of choice, which grants control of public schools to local boards and finances school operations (except teacher salaries) according to a formula based on enrollment and need (Centre for Educational Research and Innovation 1994).

A second lesson from the Chilean educational reforms of the 1980s is relevant to these experiments. Privatization and the use of exit signals do not automatically lead to educational innovation because it is not bureaucratic rules alone, or even primarily, that constrain originality and risk-taking in the classroom. Chilean municipal and private schools do not take advantage of the discretion and the authority made available to them partly because Chilean parents often do not choose schools for educational reasons. Studies of public school choice in England also find that many parents are not choosing schools on the basis of particular educational offerings, nor are schools innovating as much reform as advocates had originally hoped (Centre for

Educational Research and Innovation 1994). Simply put, parents often do not seek educational innovation. Education serves a variety of functions, only one of which is academic achievement. Although nearly all parents send their children to school in order that they learn, they assign varying importance to other priorities, such as safety, convenience, day care, familiarity with the values and social codes of their children's peers, and agreement with religious and moral teachings. In specific settings, parents willingly trade academic achievement or educational innovation for those other priorities. Exit signals and the post-welfare model seem to be more effective in promoting innovation in health care, where there is greater agreement on what medicine is supposed to achieve.

As a result, educational reforms that promote new pedagogical techniques or a greater variety of educational offerings will require focused teacher training and the deliberate establishment of new programs, such as magnet schools. In education, there is no reason to believe that the private sector will provide those options spontaneously. Recently, the Chilean Ministry of Education has launched programs that fund and reward experimental approaches, recognizing that it would have to adopt an active role if the traditional style of education in Chile, top-down with a great deal of memorization, is to change.

A third and related lesson from the Chilean reforms is that information failures will persist in a choice system. Because it is prolonged and relatively isolated, the learning process and its outcomes are extremely difficult to evaluate. In other sectors, privatization more readily promotes technological innovation and progress because results there are clearer. In Chile, for example, whatever the consequences for equity, it is clear that the introduction of market forces in health and pensions during the 1980s led to impressive investments in effective health technologies on the part of health providers and financial and business innovations on the part of pension fund managers. But neither randomized, double-blind trials nor graphs of risk and return are available for educational experiments. As a result, the assessment of school choice experiments that aim to improve educational performance by improving incentives in the sector will require more sophisticated systems for the measurement and evaluation of educational achievement. Those evaluation systems could be used, of course, to improve the mechanisms of accountability in traditional, publicly provided education as well.

A final lesson from Chile is that the design of school choice experiments should take seriously the concern that they might increase stratification by class or race. More motivated and informed parents will seek out "better" schools at the same time that those competing schools seek them. Studies of the Milwaukee program found that parents whose children applied to the choice program were more educated (especially the mothers), had somewhat higher educational expectations, and were more likely to study class materials at home with their children (Witte et al. 1994, Witte and Thorn 1996). Requiring private schools that receive vouchers or public subsidies to randomly select students if they receive more applications than they can fill, as Milwaukee does, ameliorates the problem somewhat. The Milwaukee studies show, however, that even with such a stipulation not all parents will take equal advantage of the choices available to them, which will leave some schools with a greater concentration of "at-risk" students.

For a health care system of competing private providers paid on a prospective per capita basis, measuring and predicting the health risks for providers' given pools of individuals and compensating them for the differential risks, while technically challenging, would not be impossible; however, that technique would not work in education. Because their marginal profits are lower, educational systems pool students into groups of at most a few thousand (schools), which makes risks harder to predict. More importantly, however, whereas in health care it is immaterial to a given consumer who exits from or enters into his provider's care, in education the exit and entry of peers affect a student's learning. When the students from better endowed families leave a school, the quality of education for those who remain probably declines; or even if it does not measurably decline, the school becomes a less attractive option for most parents because they believe that associating with those students is itself beneficial. If the impact and importance of peer effects were known with precision, the remaining students as well the abandoned schools might be compensated. But how exactly students learn, and the role of schools in their learning, remains mysterious.

Policy reforms, post-welfare or otherwise, must recognize the characteristics of the practices they seek to change. Education is complex because although its good is obvious, its display is unpredictable. Sometimes education appears as factual knowledge or the mastery of a skill; at other times it manifests a belief, curiosity, a habit, or the willingness to admit ignorance. And how it works, the cognitive processes that underlie it, remain poorly understood, more mysterious than the processes by which doctors heal the body. Uncertainty, and therefore disagreement, about its goals and mechanisms complicate expectations to produce it. It seems appropriate, then, to conclude with this story:

An old Jewish folktale describes the great Talmudic sage as an impoverished young man who wanted to study at one of the Jerusalem academies. He earned money by chopping wood, but barely enough money to keep himself alive, let alone pay the admission fees for the lectures. One cold winter night, when he had no money at all, Hillel climbed to the roof of the school building and listened through the skylight. Exhausted, he fell asleep and was soon covered with snow. The next morning, the assembled scholars saw the sleeping figure blocking the light. When they realized what he had been doing, they immediately admitted him to the academy, waiving the fees. It didn't matter that he was ill dressed, penniless, a recent immigrant from Babylonia, his family unknown. He was so obviously a student. (Walzer 1983, 201)

APPENDIX

A Statistical Portrait of Chilean Families with Children in School

Tables 8–17 present summary characteristics—means—for the three school types or categories of achievement level (top, middling, bottom) and for the private paid sector, as well as the results according to sector (municipal, private subsidized, private paid). The sample population in each case is all students in the sample with non-missing data for the trait in question. Because the sampling procedure gives an unbiased estimate of mean family size in the total population of school-age children, siblings are treated as distinct individuals with identical values for certain characteristics, such as household per capita income, parental education, and so on. In other words, the unit in each table is the student, not the household.

The breakdown of mean values by sector is presented for the purposes of comparison only and is not the focus of the present analysis. Although nearly all previous studies of the Chilean system emphasize distinctions between municipal and private subsidized schools and find, in the differences between their populations, evidence for stratification, the two sectors in reality differ less than is commonly believed. For reasons outlined in chapter 2, neither sector enjoys much autonomy from the Ministry of Education, and hence the divergence in behavior between the municipal and private subsidized schools, though potentially substantial, is limited in practice. A brief comparison of tables 8 and 9 shows that patterned socioeconomic differences are greater between school types than between sectors: by analyzing schools by ownership and not by levels of achievement, most writers underestimate the degree of stratification in the Chilean subsidized system.

The socioeconomic characteristics presented in table 8 establish a pattern: in general, children in top schools come from families of a higher socioeconomic level than children in middling schools, whose families in turn are slightly better endowed than children in bottom schools. The average student in a top school comes from a household with a per capita income of nearly 40,000 pesos per month, has a mother who has had more than two and a half years of secondary education and who reads an elite newspaper regularly (with a probability of 20 percent), and lives in a household with a 10 percent chance of owning a car. That per capita income figure was equal to about US$100 per month in 1993, which was about 40 percent of per capita GDP. (The mean income figures are probably all underestimates, reflecting the widespread tendency of respondents to understate their income out of fear that

Table 8. Socioeconomic Characteristics of Students in Chilean Schools, by School Achievement Level

	Bottom n=342	Middling n=408	Top n=276	Private Paid n=181
Household income per capita (in pesos per month)[a] [b]	21,563 (19,985) [n=335]	28,336 (27,291) [n=401]	39,663 (30,111) [n=258]	157,347 (130,509) [n=142]
Mother's education (years)[a]	7.8 (3.2) [n=338]	9.3 (3.2) [n=404]	10.6 (3.3) [n=277]	14.8 (3.1) [n=176]
Father's education (years)[a]	8.7 (3.6) [n=297]	9.8 (3.0) [n=344]	11.3 (3.3) [n=255]	15.7 (3.1) [n=176]
Parents are married (%)[a]	76.6	77.2	89.5	88.3
Female-headed household (%)	13.5	16.7	8.7	6.6
Age of head of household	42.9 (9.9)	43.7 (10.4)	43.4 (9.9)	46.1 (10.4)
Family reads an "elite" newspaper (%)[a]	4.7	11.3	19.2	77.9
Family owns car (%)[a]	0.9	2.9	9.1	51.3
Child is learning-disabled (%)	8.8	7.1	6.9	3.9

Source: Author.
Note: In 1993, about 400 Chilean pesos = US$1. Standard deviations are in parentheses. Subsample sizes in brackets are exceptions.
    a. Mean values are significantly different for bottom and top schools, at $p < .05$.
    b. The means test employed a logarithmic transformation of the variable.

the surveys will be used for taxation purposes. The figures do allow for an interesting comparison of relative incomes across school types, however. The car ownership figure is based on the survey question that asked whether the child ever went to school in a car belonging to the family. Although the actual rate of car ownership is probably higher, the question again permits a reasonable estimate of the relative rates across school types and sectors.)

The household of the average student in a bottom school, meanwhile, has a

Table 9. Socioeconomic Characteristics of Students in Chilean Schools, by School Sector

	Municipal n=490	Private Subsidized n=520	Private Paid n=181
Household income per capita (in pesos per month)[a][b]	25,344 (23,309) [n=474]	32,867 (29,706) [n=504]	157,347 (130,509) [n=142]
Mother's education (years)[a]	8.8 (3.5) [n=486]	9.5 (3.3) [n=516]	14.7 (3.1) [n=177]
Father's education (years)[a]	9.4 (3.4) [n=425]	10.3 (3.4) [n=453]	15.7 (3.1) [n=172]
Parents are married (%)	79.6	80.4	88.4
Female-headed household (%)	14.9	12.5	6.6
Age of head of household	43.3 (10.0)	43.4 (10.3)	46.1 (10.5)
Family reads an "elite" newspaper (%)[a]	7.3	15.0	77.9
Family owns car (%)[a]	1.2	6.7	51.4
Child is learning-disabled (%)	8.8	6.9	3.9

Source: Author.
Note: In 1993, about 400 Chilean pesos = US$1. Standard deviations are in parentheses. Subsample sizes in brackets are exceptions.
  a. Mean values are significantly different for municipal and private subsidized schools, at $p < .05$.
  b. The means test employed a logarithmic transformation of the variable.

mean per capita income of about 21,000 pesos per month, has a mother (or female guardian) who did not finish elementary school and who reads an elite newspaper regularly (with a probability of 5 percent), and has less than a 1 percent chance of owning a car. The likelihood of coming from a stable family environment, measured by the proxies of having married parents and a female head of household (a married female head of household is a cultural and legal impossibility in Chile), also increases with school level: while 77 percent of students in bottom schools live with married parents (or guardians) and 13.5 percent have a female as head of their household, the corresponding figures for top students are 88 percent and 9 percent, respectively.

Table 8 presents strong prima facie evidence for sorting by socioeconomic status in the Chilean subsidized system. The source of the sorting, whether schools are "creaming," whether families with greater endowments are more successful searchers, or whether there is such homogeneity in the schools that socioeconomic differences explain school achievement status, cannot be determined from table 8. The data strongly suggest, however, that opportunities for learning are not equal across classes in the subsidized system. The table also verifies the enormous class division between the private paid schools and the subsidized sector taken as a whole.

Tables 10 and 11 present evidence to indicate that parental participation in school life—volunteering, speaking to teachers, and so on—does not vary widely across subsidized school types or by sector. While parents in top and middling schools are more likely to belong to the leadership of the parents' association, to volunteer, and to attend parent association meetings, the differences in participation rates do not appear large. Meeting attendance is the only measure that appears significantly different between top and bottom schools. Parents in all school types, including the private paid sector, talk to teachers and principals about 7.5 to 8 times a year. Between 35 and 40 percent of parents in the subsidized sector school types volunteered at the school during the past year, while 55 percent of parents in the private paid sector volunteered. Among parents who volunteered, the mean hours worked were 17.6 in the subsidized sector and 26.7 in private paid schools (not shown in table 10).

While parental participation does not vary widely, reported search behavior does exhibit significant differences by school type. Three survey questions were asked: "How do you know if a school is good?" "Did you consider other schools for your child at the time of enrollment?" and "Why did you choose this school for your child?" Parents of top schools were significantly more likely to use specific indicators to assess school quality. The responses categorized as *specific indicators* were references to class size, teaching methods, the rate of university matriculation, SIMCE or college entrance exam test scores, the school mission statement, extracurricular activities, and foreign language classes. Parents in top schools were also more likely to have considered other possibilities at the moment of enrollment and were less likely to have chosen their child's school for nonacademic reasons. By far the most common nonacademic reason for choosing a school was nearness to the home (39.8 percent in subsidized schools, 11.1 percent in private paid). *Academic reasons* included any factor that might in some way affect achievement, including the quality of instruction, discipline, values, curriculum, religious orientation, a full day of classes, specific indicators or outcomes, and materials and resources. These results suggest that parents in top schools search more purposefully and with more focus than other parents—more of them seem to know what to look for in a school.

Table 10 suggests that parents with children in higher achieving schools are more satisfied with their children's education and that parents who think highly of their children's academic abilities are more likely to enroll them in higher achieving schools. The direction of causality probably points both ways in each case. Parents with children in top schools might be more satisfied because the schools are in fact better, or the expression of satisfaction might reflect a parent's pride in her own search efforts and thus make placement in a higher achieving school more likely. Similarly, a parent of a child in a higher achieving school might assess her child's academic level more optimistically because of faith in that school, but the children's academic level also makes it more likely that they will be accepted into a better establishment and that the parents, motivated by their children's potential, will strive to place them in a good school.

Table 10 shows a clear relationship between enrollment in a higher achieving school and having taken a matriculation exam. Top schools are in general more selective than middling and bottom schools: over 46 percent of students enrolled in them took a test to gain admission. What is striking is not only the disparity in selectivity among school types but the overall rate of admissions testing in the subsidized sector—28 percent. Although not formally illegal, admission tests in the subsidized sector are culturally and normatively proscribed. Most private subsidized school directors would deny using them, claiming that the pre-admission tests they implement serve diagnostic purposes only and that pre-enrollment interviews with parents are designed to acquaint parents with the general philosophy of the school, not to screen. Some fraction of the respondents who said their child took an exam to matriculate might have mistaken a diagnostic exam for an admissions test. It is improbable that most of them did so, however, because cross-tabulations between a child's having taken an admission test and his or her mother's having attended college, between admissions testing and a father's having attended college, and between admissions testing and family car ownership found that all subsidized sector students in the sample from the higher levels of socioeconomic background and who took admissions tests were attending top schools. Meanwhile the coefficient on a child possessing above average academic abilities as reported by parents, as well as an inter-action between having taken a test and the child possessing above average academic abilities, is not significant in either of the models. These results are consistent with the interpretation that the exams, as is widely believed, are not merely diagnostic but

Table 10. Participation, Search Techniques, and Traits of Families at the Present School, by School Achievement Level

	Bottom n=342	Middling n=408	Top n=276	Private Paid n=181
Family are leaders in the school parents' association (%)	9.1	14.0	12.7	19.3
No. of times family spoke to teacher or principal during the last year	8.0 (6.7)	7.7 (10.5)	7.8 (9.3)	7.5 (12.9)
Family volunteered at school during the last year (%)	31.5	35.5	40.6	55.2
Family attended all parents' association meetings during the last year (%)ᵃ	64.9	70.8	74.0	83.3
Family responded with specific indicators to question, "How do you know if a school is good?" (%)ᵃ	3.5	5.4	18.5	22.7
Family considered other schools before enrolling (%)ᵃ	15.2	18.1	26.8	17.1
Family chose school for nonacademic reasons (%)ᵃ	58.2	49.0	32.6	13.8
Family are "very satisfied" with child's education (%)ᵃ	60.2	64.5	73.9	88.4
Family believe their child is academically "above average" (%)ᵃ	20.8	27.9	38.4	49.2
Child took a test to enroll in school (%)ᵃ	15.4 [n=337]	27.6 [n=402]	46.1 [n=271]	81.8 [n=181]

Source: Author.
Note: Subsample sizes in brackets are exceptions. Standard deviations are in parentheses.
    a. Mean values are significantly different for municipal and private subsidized schools, at $p < .05$.

are used for selection. Most educators in Chile would acknowledge the existence of some admissions testing in the subsidized sector, but the survey results find a much wider prevalence than expected: almost half the slots in the top schools require testing prior to enrollment.

Table 11. Participation, Search Techniques, and Traits of Families at the Present School, by School Sector

	Municipal n=490	Private Subsidized n=520	Private Paid n=181
Family are leaders in the school parents' association (%)	11.2	12.7	19.3
No. of times family spoke to teacher or principal during the last year	8.1 (9.2)	7.7 (9.1)	7.5 (12.9)
Family volunteered at school during the last year (%)	38.2	35.2	55.2
Family attended all parents' association meetings during the last year (%)	66.7	71.9	83.4
Family responded with specific indicators to question, "How do you know if a school is good?" (%)[a]	4.9	11.7	22.7
Family considered other schools before enrolling (%)[a]	15.9	22.9	17.1
Family chose school for nonacademic reasons (%)[a]	57.8	40.0	13.8
Family are "very satisfied" with child's education (%)[a]	62.2	68.1	88.4
Family believe their child is academically "above average" (%)	26.5	30.6	49.2
Child took a test to enroll in school (%)[a]	17.5 [n=481]	36.8 [n=513]	81.8 [n=181]

Source: Author.

Note: Subsample sizes in brackets are exceptions. Standard deviations are in parentheses.

a. Mean values are significantly different for municipal and private subsidized schools, at p <. 05.

Tables 12 and 13 focus on the attitudes and opinions of parents. A series of questions in the survey asked interviewees to compare education to other goods, such as a good job, a good place to live, and enough money, and to respond whether they believed that education is more important, less important, or equal in impor-

Table 12. Family Attitudes and Opinions, by School Achievement Level (in percent)

	Bottom n=342	Middling n=408	Top n=276	Private Paid n=181
Family would be "very angry" or "very upset" if lost right to choose school[a]	53.5	53.7	71.4	93.3
Family believe that "if the goal is to improve the quality of education, the ministry should manage schools	83.0	84.1	84.8	65.7
Family believe education is:				
More important than a good job[a]	60.2	67.1	73.6	84.5
More important than earning a lot of money[a]	62.9	69.4	71.4	88.4
More important than religion	42.1	45.6	44.6	49.2
More important than ethnic tradition	60.5	63.7	62.7	68.0
More important than a good place to live[a]	25.1	36.0	39.1	54.1
Family believe that quality of education is more important than the problem of crime[a]	50.3	53.1	58.7	81.8
Family believe that quality of education is more important than equal access to health care	13.5	15.0	19.2	26.0

Source: Author.
   a. Mean values are significantly different for bottom and top schools, at $p < .05$.

tance to the other factor. Two separate questions asked them to compare the quality of education as a policy problem to crime and to health care, and two other queries attempted to divulge their attitudes on issues important for "choice" theory. The results show that parents in top schools seem significantly more concerned about the right to choose a school for their children. Parents in private paid schools, not surprisingly, seem to value this right even more highly; and they are least likely to exhibit faith in the Ministry of Education's capacity to improve the quality of edu-

Table 13. Family Attitudes and Opinions, by School Sector (in percent)

	Municipal n=490	Private Subsidized n=520	Private Paid n=181
Family would be "very angry" or "very upset" if lost right to choose school[a]	54.7	62.7	93.4
Family believe that "if the goal is to improve the quality of education, the ministry should manage schools	82.4	86.2	65.7
Family believe education is:			
More important than a good job	66.1	66.5	84.5
More important than earning a lot of money	66.3	67.9	88.3
More important than religion	45.6	43.3	49.2
More important than ethnic tradition	63.7	59.6	68.0
More important than a good place to live[a]	27.6	36.9	54.1
Family believe that quality of education is more important than the problem of crime	53.9	52.7	81.7
Family believe that quality of education is more important than equal access to health care	13.5	17.1	26.0

Source: Author.

a. Mean values are significantly different for municipal and private subsidized schools, at $p < .05$.

cation. Parents in all school types, however, including the private paid, chose the ministry as the body most able to improve school quality (other choices were school owners, parents, teachers, and municipal mayors). This suggests that the "mentality" of the choice system, in which localities and private agents assume responsibility for education, has not diffused well among Chilean parents. A second finding is that top parents are significantly more likely than bottom parents to believe that education is more important than a good job, earning a lot of money, and a good place to live. Because there were no significant differences across school types in the relative importance of education when compared with religion and ethnic tradition, this suggests that top parents exhibit a stronger understanding or faith in the instrumental value of education. For them, it might well provide a good job, a lot of money, and a good place to live, whereas for bottom parents a school's value is less obvious. Finally, parents in top schools are somewhat more likely to believe that educational quality is more important than other social problems, such as crime and health care.

Table 14 presents measures of household educational expenditures and transportation costs per student on the basis of school type. Although subsidized schools are by law tuition-free, they can and do charge small, limited fees on an annual or monthly basis to support school activities and the parents' association. These fees, as table 14 indicates, are not high: 25,223 Chilean pesos, the sum of average annual payments for students in top schools, was worth about US$63 in 1993. It is interesting to note that although families of top students pay more than twice as much per child in annual school fees, the payments to each subsidized school type as a fraction of household income are nearly identical: about 1 percent in 1993. Students in top schools also travel farther, use more time, and spend more to commute to their schools than students in the other subsidized schools. They are more likely to get to school in a family car and less likely to walk. These figures suggest that attending a higher achieving school requires a greater expenditure of money and time than attending a mediocre school, and that families with more disposable income and wealth are more likely to possess the requisite resources to make such an effort. The variances in annual payments by school type were unexpectedly high. An examination of the data revealed that some particularly well-off families paid sizable fees to their schools on a "voluntary" basis, or what some called "voluntary but with pressure." This raised the mean value of payments in the subsidized sector and increased their variances substantially.

Table 14 includes answers to a hypothetical question about how much parents would be willing to sacrifice if their children could attend one of the five best schools in the metropolitan area. The results indicate that parents in all school types would be willing to multiply their present payments several fold for such an opportunity.

Parents in top schools would be willing to pay the most—more than 17,000 pesos per month. Parents in all subsidized school types would be willing to pay about 8 percent of their average household income, which is almost the same fraction of household income that parents in the private paid sector currently spend.

Table 15 shows that students in private subsidized schools spend nearly four times as much in school fees as students in municipal schools, and about twice as

Table 14. Household Expenditures and Transportation per Student, by School Achievement Level

	Bottom n=342	Middling n=408	Top n=276	Private Paid n=181
Total payments to school in 1993, in pesos[a] [b]	9,319 (12,075)	13,818 (18,261)	25,223 (36,635)	624,330 (352,535)
As fraction of household income	0.010	0.011	0.013	0.096
Weekly cost of transportation to and from school, in pesos[a] [b]	163 (466)	289 (607)	703 (1,061)	2,335 (3,172)
No. of blocks to school[a]	11.6 (15.4)	14.2 (18.0)	19.2 (21.6)	25.2 (20.5)
No. of minutes spent traveling to and from school[a]	13.2 (11.9)	14.2 (11.9)	17.9 (15.8)	18.7 (14.9)
Student travels by car (%)[a]	0.9	2.9	9.1	51.4
Student walks to school (%)[a]	73.7	61.8	43.8	14.4
Pesos per month family are willing to spend if child could attend one of the five best schools in the metropolitan area[b]	7,086 (8,287) [n=294]	9,672 (10,734) [n=365]	17,128 (50,532) [n=247]	65,146 (38,007) [n=152]
As fraction of household income	0.080	0.081	0.085	0.122
No. of minutes in travel time family would accept if child could attend one the five best schools in the metropolitan area	42.5 (16.2) [n=320]	41.1 (16.8) [n=385]	40.3 (16.0) [n=255]	28.2 (11.6) [n=163]

Source: Author.
Note: Standard deviations are in parentheses. Subsample sizes in brackets are exceptions.
 a. Mean values are significantly different for bottom and top schools, at p < .05.
 b. The means test employed a logarithmic transformation of the variable.

much as a fraction of household income. This reflects the existence of the *finan* *ciamiento compartido* (shared finance) system, which permits schools to charge fee on a voluntary basis, in private subsidized schools. Chilean law now permits suc fees in municipal secondary schools as well, and the differences in the sectoral mean will probably decline in the coming years. Critics who are concerned about th

Table 15. Household Expenditures and Transportation per Student, by School Sector

	Municipal n=490	Private Subsidized n=520	Private Paid n=181
Total payments to school in 1993, in pesos[a] [b]	6,682 (7,791)	23,626 (31,440)	624,33C (352,535)
As fraction of household income	0.007	0.015	0.096
Weekly cost of transportation to and from school, in pesos[a] [b]	233 (616)	470 (857)	2,335 (3,172)
No. of blocks to school	13.7 (19.9)	14.7 (16.1)	25.2 (20.5)
No. of minutes spent traveling to and from school	13.6 (12.3)	15.4 (13.3)	18.8 (14.9)
Student travels by car (%)[a]	1.2	6.7	51.4
Student walks to school (%)[a]	70.0	54.6	14.4
Pesos per month family are willing to spend if child could attend one of the five best schools in the metropolitan area[b]	8,226 (9,693) [n=420]	13,427 (37,363) [n=474]	65,146 (38,007) [n=152]
As fraction of household income	0.079	0.085	0.122
No. of minutes in travel time parents would accept if child could attend one of the five best schools in the metropolitan area	42.0 (16.4) [n=457]	40.5 (16.5) [n=487]	28.2 (11.6) [n=163]

Source: Author.
Note: Standard deviations are in parentheses. Subsample sizes in brackets are exceptions.
    a. Mean values are significantly different for municipal and private subsidized schools, at p < .05.
    b. The means test employed a logarithmic transformation of the variable.

equity effects of the new system fear that the differences in school type means, how-ever, might grow. In some cases, parents of children attending the same schools in the survey differed on whether the fees they paid were "voluntary," "voluntary but with pressure," or "obligatory." This suggests that schools do not make it clear that monthly fees are voluntary. By law, no monthly fees in the subsidized sector can be obligatory. The fact that some parents call them so, or confess that they pay volun-tarily but under some duress, seems to confirm the concerns of some critics who fear that the voluntary nature of the "shared finance" system is inoperable in practice.

Finally, tables 16 and 17 present several measures of parental information about schools. The results together establish a positive correlation between being informed and enrolling one's children in a higher achieving school. Although the information measured, what parents know once their child is enrolled in a school, is not exactly the same as ex ante information that parents use when searching, the difference between the two is probably not substantial. The first indicator, in row one, is based on a question that asked the interviewees to name the five best subsidized schools in the metropolitan region. Their answer was scored correct if they succeeded in nam-ing two schools whose SIMCE scores lay in the upper third for the region. Parents in top schools outperformed all others, including parents of children in the private paid sector, who, unsurprisingly, were not particularly well informed about school quality in the subsidized sector. The second question, in row two, asked the same question but at the level of the municipality. Results for this question were calcu-lable only for elementary schools. Questions in the third and fourth rows gave the interviewees a list of schools and asked them to order the schools by quality. The SIMCE scores of the schools or pairs of schools they were asked to order differed by, on average, 12.2 points. The idea was that even if SIMCE scores do not assess qual-ity perfectly, large differences in scores ought to correlate with differences in other measures available to parents, such as reputation at the local level. Rows five and six show that very few parents actually knew the SIMCE score for their child's school—many of them, despite the information campaigns launched by the authorities over the last several years, did not even know what the SIMCE is. The last row asked par-ents to specify whether the school they attended is municipal, privately subsidized, privately paid, or corporation.

The data indicate not only that being informed varies by school type but that the overall quality of information in the subsidized sector is poor. Only 39.1 percent of parents in that sector could name two schools anywhere in Greater Santiago whose test scores were in the upper third, only 17.2 percent could order a list of schools in the region whose SIMCE scores varied widely (where the differences were less than 10 points answers that interposed the schools were scored correct), and only

27.2 percent could name the top school in their municipality from a list of fiv choices. These informational failings are critical problems for a "choice" system. information is poor, schools that are innovating and attempting to improve the qua ity of instruction might elicit no response from parents and might even experienc a drop in enrollment requests; mediocre or deteriorating schools, if they advertis slyly, might be able to gain students and, therefore, revenues. The incentive structur of the system depends on good and widespread information; but that, as this surve documents, is absent in Chile.

Table 16. Family's Information Concerning School Quality, by School Achievement Level (in percent)

	Bottom n=342	Middling n=408	Top n=276	Private Paid n=18
Family could name two subsidized schools in the metropolitan region whose test scores were in the upper third for the region[a]	26.3	38.4	56.9	53.0
Family of elementary school students could name two schools in the comuna whose scores were in the upper third for the comuna[a]	30.9 [n=259]	42.6 [n=296]	51.3 [n=230]	45.3 [n=139
Family correctly ordered a group of four subsidized schools in the region according to test score	16.1	17.9	17.8	12.2
Family correctly named the top subsidized schools in the comuna from a list of five, including their child's school[a]	21.1	27.7	33.7	n.a
Family knew the SIMCE test score for their child's school (within two points)	0.0	0.0	0.72	1.11
Family knew what the SIMCE is[a]	57.9	63.5	70.3	87.8
Family identified the sector to which their child's school belongs	88.3	81.4	87.3	92.3

Source: Author.
Note: Subsample sizes in brackets are exceptions.
   a. Mean values are significantly different for bottom and top schools, at p < .05.

Table 17. Family's Information Concerning School Quality, by School Sector (in percent)

	Municipal n=408	Private Subsidized n=520	Private Paid n=181
Family could name two subsidized schools in the metropolitan region whose test scores were in the upper third for the region[a]	31.4	46.7	53.0
Family of elementary school students could name two schools in the *comuna* whose scores were in the upper third for the *comuna*[a]	34.6 [n=382]	47.6 [n=403]	45.3 [n=138]
Family correctly ordered a group of four subsidized schools in the region according to test score	16.9	17.7	12.2
Family correctly named the top subsidized schools in the *comuna* from a list of five, including their child's school	26.5	26.9	n.a.
Family knew the SIMCE test score for their child's school (within two points)	0.0	0.39	1.11
Family knew what the SIMCE is	62.2	65.6	87.8
Family identified the sector to which their child's school belongs[a]	94.5	80.1	92.3

Source: Author.

Note: Subsample sizes in brackets are exceptions.

a. Mean values are significantly different for municipal and private subsidized schools, at $p < .05$.

NOTES

Chapter 1. The Contemporary Movement to Reform the Social Sectors

1. "Economic issues overwhelmed all other policy priorities in the 1980s. In contrast, the 1990s—with new imperatives for social equity, growth and environmental sustainability, as well as for political and state reform—seems to be a new era in the scope of the policy agenda" (Bradford 1994).

2. Mexico regionalized financial and managerial control of basic schooling to ministerial state delegations starting in 1978 and subsequently attempted to turn over control to the states. In the mid-1970s, Argentina's military regime broadened existing decentralization in several sectors, including health and education, a process that resulted in the transfer of preschool, primary and adult education to the provinces by the mid-1980s. In Brazil, state governments and, to a lesser extent, its municipalities have been involved in the provision of social services, including primary education, for decades, both directly and through the oversight of associated autonomous corporations. In health care, Brazil's national health system contracts out the majority of health care provision to private providers.

3. Peru has been building a system of individually capitalized social security pensions. In 1992 the government proposed an outright transfer of state schools to private hands and a financing design based on the use of vouchers. A related program aims to expand community participation in Peru's local health posts. Bolivia's health ministry has transferred financial power to regional "health units" and to ninety-four local health districts. A 1993 Bolivian proposal would have decentralized administrative and financial powers in education to the local level and suggested a probable or a possible privatization of the nation's schools. In social security, Bolivia has initiated a program of "social capitalization" in the privatization of state enterprises to transform the nation's underfunded pension system. Colombia launched a systemic health care reform in 1993 that brought public and private providers of health care, as well as public and private health financiers, into direct competition. Colombia has also attempted experiments that provide for vouchers and the local control of education in Bogotá and other cities. In Venezuela, as a result of the Decentralization Law of 1990, local governments can request the transfer of funds and personnel in order to manage social programs, economic development, and infrastructure projects independently. Argentina passed legislation to create individually capitalized, privately managed and owned pension funds in 1993; and it is currently considering a plan that would permit individuals to choose among competing social insurance funds. In 1995 Mexico initiated a program to expand the powers of state institutions to manage health care; and in 1998 the Mexican government expected to approve regulations permitting consumers to opt out of the national social security institute and establish contracts with private health insurers (Torres and Mathur 1996; Medici et al. 1997; World Bank 1995).

Chapter 2. The Theory and Practice of School Choice in Chile

1. Although Enlightenment-inspired and hierarchical, the Chilean system was not as successful as the French. Former Minister of Education Gonzalo Vial dryly commented, "That French minister who knew everything that was going on in every classroom in the country was not the minister of education in Chile. The minister of education in Chile and the Chilean ministry did not know anything about what was going on in any of the classrooms in his country" (Cox 1985, 120).

2. Núñez 1989 attributes the failure of the plan of 1927 to opposition from the chiefs of the educational hierarchy, including the university professors, secondary school teachers, and normal school professors, who benefited from the centralization of power. Núñez does not, however, make the crucial point about the failure of decentralization efforts before 1980: none of them challenged the dominance of political parties in Chilean education, and the teacher union leaders were party members first and educators second.

3. The history is taken from Cox 1984 and Labarca 1939.

4. It is evident, of course, that private sector outcomes can be suboptimal as well. Stiglitz 1989 and Shapiro and Willig 1990 argue that there is no theoretical reason why public ownership must be less efficient than private, given optimally designed regulation and taxes and perfect information. They point out, however, that in practice competitive environments and sufficient information are more commonly found in the private sector.

5. Cheema and Rondinelli 1983 call the last form "devolution." Other writers use "devolution" for the delegation of powers to semiautonomous agencies.

6. While some writers, especially those assessing privatization in the former Eastern Bloc countries, limit the concept to the sale of nationalized firms and other state assets, this analysis adopts a wider definition that links privatization to a broader policy movement. See Gormley 1991; Suleiman and Waterbury 1990.

7. The literature on educational choice is now voluminous. For criticisms, see Elmore and Fuller 1996, Henig 1994, Levin 1990, and Carnegie Foundation 1992. For studies of educational choice in the international context, see Cummings and Riddell 1993; James 1987; Johnson 1990.

8. Based on an interview with Juan Carlos Méndez, June 9, 1994, and on the account in Espinoza and González 1993.

9. *Subsidiariedad* was the doctrine, appropriated and championed by the military government, that the rights of private agents ought to supersede the state's prerogatives wherever possible. It was to serve as an ideological bulwark against a return to a socialized economy.

10. Decreto Ley No. 3476, August 29, 1980. The great majority of the leases were written for ninety-nine years. Decree 1-3063 had in fact permitted either a leasing arrangement or an outright transfer, and the leases were eventually and gradually modified to become permanent transfers of property to the municipalities. It is interesting to note that the original leases for the transfer of primary health clinics to the municipalities had five-year terms. As a result, the municipalization of education rested and continues to rest on much firmer ground than that of primary health care. The explanation for the different terms of duration includes not only the technical views of the neoliberal economists but also the greater strength of the Ministry of Health relative to the Ministry of Education, and of doctors to school teachers.

11. Méndez, in the interview of June 9, 1994, called the law "an expensive piece of leg-

islation." In Espinoza and González 1993, Alfredo Prieto states that the law was the factor that "most hurried the municipalization." The law itself was Decreto Ley No. 2327, September 1, 1978.

12. The 87 percent figure comes from Castañeda 1992, while the estimate of 84 percent is in Hevia 1982.

13. Although Chile's Colegio de Profesores, the professional association of teachers, is not legally recognized as a union, it effectively behaves as one; and this study will for convenience refer to it as such.

14. Such recognition is based on a number of characteristics: the school must have a juridical owner or "patron;" the patron or, if it is a corporate entity, its legal representative must possess a high school diploma; and the school must adhere to the ministry's plans and programs of study. See Ley No. 18.962, "Ley Orgánica Constitucional de Enseñanza," March 7, 1990, Article 21.

15. Ley Orgánica Constitucional de Enseñanza (Ley No. 18.962, March 7, 1990); Decreto con Fuerza de Ley No. 5, March 9, 1993.

16. Profit-maximizing behavior was the most scandalous element of the new system for many Chileans. Even in its most innocuous forms, such as newspaper advertisements for the sale of schools that listed property, enrollments, and the number of teachers under contract, it was shocking to segments of a citizenry for whom the idea of making money from children sounded nefarious. One practice associated with attendance-based subventions, giving out prizes or certificates to students with the best attendance records, arguably had educational value; but this was tainted by widespread reports that schools were falsifying attendance rates. Several private subsidized schools quickly learned ruses to attract students. There were reports of schools that were giving away shoes (first the left one in March, then the right one at the end of the year in December), adopting school uniforms to mimic elite private paid schools, and using foreign words or saints in the school name to appear prestigious or pious. Some were allegedly lowering standards and students' test scores at the secondary level, which is not obligatory in Chile, to avoid losing students to the work force (*El Mercurio*, April 22, 1983; Magendzo et al. 1988, esp. 121–37, 187–201).

17. Decreto 1835, December 30, 1986. A pair of excerpts illustrate the degree of detail required:

> The angle of vision of the student seated in front of the blackboard should be a minimum of 30 degrees, measured from the most unfavorable place in the room for a student to occupy, to the extreme opposite end of the blackboard.
>
> The teacher's room [for elementary education should have] a minimum of 18 square meters in locales with five to nine classrooms and a two meter increment for each additional classroom.

18. Instructivo Ministerio No. 6, May 1985. Private subsidized schools, though tuition-free by law, were permitted to charge small monthly fees, called *derechos escolares*, a fraction of which returned to the state in the form of subvention deductions. When applied to private subsidized elementary schools in 1989 and municipal schools in 1993, this practice would be called *financiamiento compartido*, described in chapter 4.

19. Former subsecretary (1984–1988) and minister (1989–1990) René Salamé said that the technical-pedagogical units, which develop curricula, pedagogical techniques, and grading

standards, were stifling innovation and pedagogical creativity in the schools (interview with René Salamé, July 19, 1994). The decree mentioned is Decreto No. 1049, September 22, 1978.

20. Decreto No. 2057, August 9, 1979, names the nine required types of documentation and forbids the maintenance of any others; Decreto No. 2088, August 14, 1979, specifies the number of tests to be administered; Decreto No. 1070, September 26, 1978, is one of many documents describing the required 1–7 grading scale. The plans of study are modified in several places, including Decreto No. 2036, December 15, 1978, for elementary education, and Decreto No. 300, December 1981, for secondary education. Personnel rankings are described in modifications of the Ley de Carrera Docente, such as Decreto No. 1084, September 1978. Decreto No. 10274, December 29, 1981, concerns the naming of schools; and the dress code is found in Decreto No. 2028, December 11, 1978. Subsequently, in Decreto No. 728/79, Modificación No. 1, June 10, 1981, sartorial liberties were expanded: principals were permitted to select the color of their boys' ties.

21. Aedo and Larrañaga 1994 summarizes the ministry's data on school characteristics and the differences between municipal and private subsidized schools.

22. The Contraloría General de la República ruled in Dicatamen No. 61,944/82 that although municipal teachers no longer have civil servant status, they remain "state officials" and cannot form unions (while teachers in private subsidized schools may). A statement of the Tribunal Constitucional, which also prohibited the creation of new municipal corporations, ruled similarly (Controlaría General de la República, Dictamen sobre el Proyecto de Ley Orgánica Constitucional de Municipios, February 29, 1988).

23. These were the findings of a corporation established in 1980 to help municipalities assume management of the schools. Based on an interview with the head of that corporation, Orezón Moya, July 5, 1994.

24. Interview with María Teresa Infante, May 27, 1994.

25. Studies of decentralization in Chile abound. See, for instance, Borja et al. 1987; Bagioli 1994; Raczynski and Serrano 1988; World Bank 1992.

26. Gustavo Cuadro, Division of Planning and Budget, Ministry of Education, Santiago, paper presented in an internal seminar on July 29, 1994.

27. Colonel Juan Deichler Guzmán, alcalde of Quinta Normal, cited in Politzer 1985, 32.

28. An order from the ministry of interior, Oficio Reservado (secreto) 1766, May 28, 1986, ordered a gradual reduction in teaching personnel. More specific municipal plans were made in secret, but one for the city of Valparaiso was leaked. See the unauthored articles in the underground teachers' journal, *El Pizarrón* (1986). Although little documentation remains from the military government, it is common knowledge that the Ministry of Interior generally ordered the alcaldes to hire and fire teaching personnel. See, for instance, "Un Autogol Difícil" (*El Mercurio*, October 3, 1993).

29. In a nonrandom sample of schools in Santiago, Espínola finds little innovation. She observes that to the extent that Chilean schools are using the flexibility now available to them, they are actually utilizing it to decrease graduation requirements. See Espínola 1993, 391.

30. Decreto Ley 18.134, June 1982, established an unindexed unit of account "specific to education" equal to 95 percent of the value of the general unit of account, the UTM. The Ministry of Finance chose to readjust wages in the public sector seven times between 1982

and September 1987, in increments ranging from 5 percent to 17 percent. In 1988, the government created a new unit of account, the *unidad de subvención educacional* (USE), linked to a new annual indexation mechanism, which amounted to an increase equal to 80 percent of the rise in a consumer price index whenever that index rose by more than 15 percent. In 1991 the democratic government would fully index the subventions on an annual basis, as well as link them to increases in wages in the public sector, on which the Congress votes each December. The Aylwin government did not attempt, however, to recover immediately the total value that the USE enjoyed prior to the 1982 deindexation. The result of the military government's deindexation was that total government spending on education fell some 20 percent in real terms between 1982 and 1983 and stayed near that level until 1992, when it would finally return to 1981 values. See Magendzo et al. 1988, 95; Infante and Schiefelbein 1992, 7.

31. Calculated on the basis of data in Montt and Serra 1994, 16; and Ministerio de Educación 1992.

32. Interview with Nelson Salinas, SUBDERE, July 28, 1994.

33. The ministry counts all education professionals, whether in the classroom or in the district office, when calculating the ratio. See Ministerio de Educación 1994.

34. See Ministerio de Educación 1994, 7; Montt and Serra 1994, 71. The ministry report finds that the rate of "surplus" seemed to be declining from 1993 to 1994, however. The number of contracted teacher hours fell 0.9 percent while enrollment rose 2.4 percent. The report attributes the recent results to the SUBDERE's program to help cover the severance pay of teachers close to retirement.

35. The Estatuto Docente was amended in 1995 to permit municipalities to reduce their teaching staffs according to Annual Plans for the Development of Municipal Education (PADEMs). The amendments also created a National System for the Evaluation of Performance (SNED), which would reward the schools whose gains on the SIMCE test were among the top 25 percent in the country. Both the PADEMs and the SNED are in their initial phase of implementation (Cox 1997).

36. Decreto 442, September 25, 1985; interview with René Salamé, July 19, 1994. Although this restriction on private school growth was included in a 1980 decree, it was not enforced until the 1985 decree reiterated the point.

37. Ley 18.372, December 17, 1984, cited in Magendzo et al. 1988, 67. The law retracted the liberty of employers to fire workers without severance pay.

38. Ley No. 18.190, December 1982; Ley No. 18.21, 1983; and Ley No. 18.267, 1983. All are cited in Frontaura 1985, 271.

39. The military regime prohibited the application of surveys to schools and carefully guarded the entrances to many educational establishments. See Núñez 1984, chaps. 2, 17; Magendzo et al. 1988, 82–89. These restrictions are described in more detail in chapter 4.

Chapter 3. Stratification in the Chilean Educational System

1. I would like to acknowledge Estelle James for her helpful comments on these ideas and research strategies.

2. There exists a substantial literature on the question, but the absence of systemwide panel data makes it difficult for any report to establish a definitive, empirically based evaluation. For reports by reform advocates, see, for example, Castañeda 1992; Matte and Sancho

1991; Jofré 1988. For mixed or critical accounts, see, for example, Schiefelbein 1991; Espínola 1995; Parry 1994; Núñez 1984; Winkler and Rounds 1996; Magendzo et al. 1988. For an account from officials in the Ministry of Education, see Montt and Serra 1994.

3. Parry 1993 finds evidence for grade inflation in a sample of fifty schools in ten municipalities in Greater Santiago.

4. See, for instance, Matte and Sancho 1993.

5. For a discussion of the analogy to health care, see Elmore 1990. On peer effects, see Henderson 1978.

6. When an elementary school did not have a 1992 fourth-year score (a school offering classes only from the sixth year and up, for example), a SIMCE math score from the 1994 eighth-year exam was used in its stead; and the school's type was determined, of course, using percentiles from that 1994 exam. Because the ministry did not have values for the 33rd and 67th percentiles for 1992 results (and was unlikely to obtain them soon because it was involved in a dispute with the firm it had contracted to analyze the test results), these values were estimated on the basis of the scores of schools in the sample. This should not affect the results of this analysis because the exact value of the cutoff points is not crucial for the results that follow, only the notion that there exist different types of schools in the subsidized sector. For convenience, this analysis uses SIMCE math scores to categorize schools, but the results would not have been affected had the Spanish or the average of the math and Spanish scores been employed: the linear correlation between math and Spanish scores is greater than $\rho = .95$. Of the students in the sample, 342 were enrolled in bottom schools, 408 in middling schools, 276 in top schools, and 181 in the private paid sector. Sixteen students in the sample attended schools for which no SIMCE scores were available—in most cases these were special education schools in which the test was not administered.

7. Estimating family car ownership on the basis of the percentage of children who commuted to school in a family car results in an underestimate. It does not include, for example, families who own cars but who live close enough to school for children to walk, or families who own cars but in which parents cannot drive children to school. Unfortunately, it was the only indicator of assets available in the questionnaire. Nevertheless, the measure correlates strongly with other predictors of social class, such as income and education. Because it is likely that excluded car-owning families are evenly distributed with respect to the independent variables of interest, the use of the variable does not bias the principal findings of this study.

8. The findings of the model appeared robust to various specifications. An ordered logit estimate using the three school types found similar results: all of the variables individually significant in the multinomial logit top/bottom equation retained their Wald-test significance, and the p-value on using specific measures of school quality fell to 0.03 for that same equation. Another estimation limited the sample to students in elementary school. Again all variables individually significant in the multinomial logit top/bottom equation retained their Wald-test significance, and the p-value on father's having attended some college fell to 0.04. Other specifications included all first-order interaction terms. None added significant predictive power to the models.

9. An examination of the distributions found, however, that although skewnesses and kurtoses varied, differences in the distributions were not enormous. For example, of the fourteen distributions implied in table 6, eight had standard deviations of between 0.25 and 0.40 of their means, and the remaining six had standard deviations between 0.5 and 0.75 of their means.

10. The most popular correction for the problem of clustering is the use of Huber standard errors, which handle the design effect of the clustering but do not resolve the issue of potentially biased coefficients. A binomial logit model estimating the odds of top school attendance relative to the odds of bottom or middling school attendance was computed, and the standard errors with and without Huber corrections were compared. Some of the Huber standard errors were smaller than the corresponding ungrouped errors while others were larger, which is probably a reflection of the inability of the Huber corrections to produce unbiased estimators with heteroscedastic models such as the logit. In any case, the Huber standard errors differed from the ungrouped errors by less than 0.1 percent on average, and all of the originally significant coefficients retained their z-test statistical significance in the Huber estimation, which suggests that the problem of intrafamily effects is probably not grave in this case. Another way to handle the clustering problem is to reduce the sample to one that contains one randomly selected student per household. When this was done, the sample size fell from 850 to 575; and family car, having married parents, using specific indicators in the search, attending meetings, and the sense of entitlement lost significance. This outcome probably owes more to the loss of degrees of freedom than to clustering effects in the original sample.

Chapter 4. The Politics of Post-Welfare Reforms in Education

1. A note on documentation: not many of the military regime's letters, memoranda, and internal orders survived. Military officials purportedly burned most of what remained when they left office. In addition, the fact that the regime's decision-making procedures were informal and highly personalized and that it had little need to explain itself to critics meant that its deliberations often went unrecorded. Iván Núñez, superintendent of education under Allende and the author of dozens of books and articles on the history of Chilean education, said he "looked through the cabinets with the eyes of an historian" when he assumed his office in the ministry in 1990, but could find "absolutely nothing" (interview, January 25, 1994). This study, like others before it, weaves together a narrative and an explanation on the basis of the documents available.

2. Individuals and organisms of the Church were among the only ones who, in the eyes of the junta, possessed the probity and the legitimacy to escape repression. Most famously, religious leaders severely criticized the regime's human rights violations; but they were also the first to denounce its educational policies publicly. Jesuits in particular took the lead in that area. See Cariola 1979, 1980; Bigo 1979.

3. Several writers make this point. See Sigmund 1977 and Valenzuela 1978. The most comprehensive history of the ENU is Farrell 1986, who writes: "The ENU dispute reinforced the perception that this was a government that could not govern and could not be trusted to abide by the constitutional and legal norms even in a matter so sensitive as the education of children. It frightened and alienated many of the remaining middle sectors whose support, or at least neutrality, was essential to the survival of the regime under the existing parliamentary system. It brought the two remaining major neutral institutions, the Church and the armed forces, into opposition. With the internally divided military still officially neutral, whose highest-ranking officers were committed constitutionalists, the ENU dispute legitimized the open expression of political dissent and lack of confidence in the government" (241).

4. Criticizing inconsistencies and mistaken policies in the education sector, Magendzo

refers to the regime's method as "trial and error." That would be right but for the addition that the object of the trial was itself unclear (Magendzo et al. 1988). Maria Teresa Infante acknowledged the junta's lack of interest in educational policy, confessing that working in a marginalized field sometimes led one to feel like a "second class citizen" in the government (interview, May 27, 1994).

5. "Directiva Presidencial para la Educación," Santiago, mimeo, March 1979. In a presidential letter to Minister of Education Gonzalo Vial that accompanied the Directive, Pinochet wrote that "the possibility that the state will expand its educational activities even more should be considered unlikely," and that the support of the private sector "will be stimulated energetically." He mentioned a "new institutionality" in which "local communities" would once again be in possession of intermediary institutions, such as Parents Associations and Student Centers. See "Educación Chilena" 1979.

6. This was an example of the argument in Cox 1991, who contends that authority for educational decision making under the military regime shifted back and forth between educational and economic "voices."

7. Arriagada et al. 1979. Juan Carlos Méndez, who had directed Arriagada to prepare a study on educational decentralization, discounted the relevance of this document during an interview on June 9, 1994. Another senior official during the military regime said that the recommendations of the Arriagada document were not accepted because of the need for "unipersonal responsibilities" at the time. See Espinoza and González 1993, 112.

8. The story is recounted in the comments of diputado Felipe Valenzuela (PDC), in *Historia de Ley* 1992, 2255. The patronage in Antofagasta's educational system was notorious. Until the Ministry of Interior, Subsecretariat of Regional Development, review of 1993, Santiago officials had no idea that Antofagasta listed over eighty educational administrators on its payroll. Other larger municipalities were getting by with six or seven administrators. (Interviews in the SUBDERE: Samuel Garrido, July 27, 1994; Nelson Salinas, July 28, 1994.) Like fifty-four other municipalities, including some of the largest ones in the country, it managed its schools and clinics with a private corporation, which gave it much more legal flexibility in hiring and firing than the municipal departments of education, which the 270 or so other remaining municipalities utilized. Although the neoliberal reformers of the early 1980s had believed that private sector, rather than governmental, jurisdiction would improve management efficiency, municipalities with private corporations were running some of the highest municipal deficits, probably as a result of patronage opportunities.

9. For example, diputado Sergio Ojeda Uribe (PDC) argued that recentralizing the schools would require a constitutional amendment (*Historia de Ley* 1992, 2294), as did the leading Chilean daily, *El Mercurio* (May 8, 1994, A20). René Salamé, on the other hand, who was the lead author of the LOCE, believed that a constitutional amendment would not be necessary (interview, July 19, 1994).

10. There was considerable debate in the Congress concerning the authority to establish the size of municipal teaching staffs. Lagos argued that because central government funds were at stake (subventions come from the treasury, after all), the ministry should possess final authority. Several members of the opposition used neoliberal rhetoric to argue that municipalities should control the size of staffs; but because at the time most of the alcaldes retained ties to the opposition, opportunities for patronage must have motivated their arguments as well. The law finally settled on a compromise: the municipalities and the provincial directorates of the ministry would jointly determine the size of the staffs. This compromise came

under fire when in 1993 it became apparent that staff sizes were increasing much faster than enrollments.

11. See Comite Técnico 1994. Another sign of the government's renewed interest in implementing post-welfare incentives was the appointment of an individual who endorsed direct subsidies to demand, or vouchers, to the post of chief of planning and budget for the Ministry of Education (González 1993).

12. For instance, when asked what steps were needed to improve education in Chile, the chair of the education committee of the lower house of Congress (the Cámara), Jose Miguel Ortíz (PDC), though endorsing municipalization, did not refer to competition or to incentive structures (interview, July 12, 1994).

13. Pedro Henríquez, formerly chief of planning and budget for the Ministry of Education under Lagos and Arrate and a key architect of the language of the Estatuto Docente, attributed the government's underestimation of the rigidities that would be created under the Estatuto Docente to inexperience and confusion (interview, November 12, 1993).

14. The argument draws on Thelen and Steinmo 1992.

15. In the 1994 national directorate, for example, the breakdown by party was: five Christian Democrats (PDC), three Communists (PC), two Radicals (PR), one Socialist (PS), one National Renovation (RN), one Democratic Independent Union (UDI), and one independent. As in most political and quasipolitical organizations in Chile, officials in the Colegio de Profesores are elected on the basis of lists that group together individuals with similar party affiliations or whose parties have made pacts.

16. Enrique Larré (RN), Eugenio Cantuarias (UDI), Claudio Rodriguez (RN), Juan Masferrer Pellizzari (UDI), Jorge Morales Adriasola (RN), Jorge Ulloa Aguillón (UDI), Luis Navarrete Carvacho (RN), and Carlos Valarce Medina (RN) all spoke on behalf of the teachers and offered the amendments listed above (*Historia de Ley* 1992).

17. Lagos commented, "We are firmly convinced of the need to decentralize. What we will have to address at some point is whether the municipality is the appropriate level for it, since municipalities are quite different from one another" (*Historia de Ley* 1992, 2246).

REFERENCES

Aedo I., Cristián, and Osvaldo J. Larrañaga. 1994. "Educación Privada versus Pública en Chile: Calidad Y Sesgo de Selección." Santiago: ILADES.

Angell, Alan, and Carol Graham. 1995. "Can Social Sector Reform Make Adjustment Sustainable and Equitable? Lessons from Chile and Venezuela." *Journal of Latin American Studies* 27, (February).

Arrigada, Patricio, et al. 1979. *Descentralización de la Gestión Educacional en Chile.* Santiago: Ministerio de Hacienda.

Bagioli G., Raúl. 1994. "Organización Interna de las Municipalidades: Descripción General y Comentarios." *Estudios Municipales* 3. Santiago: CPU.

Bahl, R. W., and J. F. Linn. 1992. *Urban Public Finance in Developing Countries.* New York: Oxford University Press.

Bennett, Robert J., ed. 1990. *Decentralization, Local Governments, and Markets: Towards a Post-Welfare Agenda.* New York: Oxford University Press.

Bennett, Robert J., ed. 1994. *Local Government and Market Decentralization.* New York: United Nations University Press.

Bermudez, J. 1975. "Sistema educacional y requerimientos del desarrollo nacional: La educación chilena en el período 1964–1974." Santiago: mimeo.

Bigo, Pierre. 1979. "La Función Subsidiaria del Estado." *Mensaje* 281 (August).

Borja, Jordi, et al., eds. 1987. *Descentralización del Estado: Movimiento Social y Gestión Local.* Santiago: FLACSO.

Bradford, Colin I., Jr. 1994. "Redefining the Role of the State: Political Process, State Capacity and the New Agenda in Latin America." In Colin I. Bradford, Jr., ed., *Redefining the State in Latin America.* Paris: OECD.

Buchanan, James M. 1968. *The Demand and Supply of Public Goods.* Chicago: Rand McNally.

———. 1975. "Public Finance and Public Choice." *National Tax Journal* 28 (December): 383–94.

Buchanan, James M., Robert D. Tollison, and Gordon Tullock, eds. 1980. *Toward a Theory of Rent-Seeking Society.* College Station: Texas A & M University Press.

Buchanan, James M., and R. E. Wagner. 1977. *Democracy in Deficit.* New York: Academic Press.

Calvo, C. 1984. "Taxi-teachers in Chile." Ph.D. diss., Stanford University.

Cariola, Patricio. 1979. "Privatización, Subsidiariedad, y Libertad de Enseñanza." *Cuadernos de Educación* 88 (August).

———. 1980. "Municipalización de la Educación Pública." *Cuadernos de Educación* 98 (August).

Carnegie Foundation for the Advancement of Teaching. 1992. *School Choice: A Special Report.* Princeton, N.J.: Carnegie Foundation.

Carr, David K., and Ian D. Littman. 1993. *Excellence in Government: Total Quality Management in the 1990s*. Arlington: Coopers and Lybrand.

Castañeda, Tarsicio. 1992. *Combating Poverty: Innovative Social Reforms in Chile During the 1980s*. San Francisco: International Center for Economic Growth.

Centre for Educational Research and Innovation, 1994. Paris: OECD.

Cheema, G. Shabbir, and Dennis A. Rondinelli, eds. 1983. *Decentralization and Development: Policy Implementation in Developing Countries*. London: Sage Publications.

Chubb, John E., and Terry M. Moe. 1990. *Politics, Markets, and America's Schools*. Washington, D.C.: Brookings Institution.

Clotfelter, Charles T., and Helen F. Ladd. 1996. "Recognizing and Rewarding Success in Public Schools." In Helen F. Ladd, ed., *Holding Schools Accountable: Performance-Based Reform in Education*, 23–64. Washington, D.C.: Brookings Institution.

Coleman, James S., Thomas Hoffer, and Sally Kilgore. 1982. *High School Achievement: Public, Private, and Catholic Schools Compared*. New York: Basic Books.

Collier, David, ed. 1979. *The New Authoritarianism in Latin America*. Princeton: Princeton University Press.

Comando de Institutos Militares. 1974. "Circular para regular el Funcionamiento de los Establecimientos Educacionales del Gran Santiago." Cited in José Joaquín Brunner, "El Diseño Autoritario de la Educación," *FLACSO Documento de Trabajo No. 86*. Santiago: FLACSO, November 1979.

Comer, James. 1989. *A Conversation Between James Comer and Ronald Edmonds: Fundamentals of Effective School Improvement*. Dubuque, Ia.: Kendall/Hunt.

Comite Técnico Asesor del Diálogo Nacional Sobre La Modernización de la Educación Chilena, Designado por S. E. El Presidente de la República. 1994. *Los Desafíos de la Educación Chilena Frente Al Siglo 21*. Santiago, September 9.

Concertación de Partidos por la Democracia. 1989. "Programa de Gobierno." Santiago, 1989.

Coons, John E., and Stephen D. Sugarman. 1978. *Education by Choice: The Case for Family Control*. Berkeley: University of California Press.

Cox D., Cristián. 1984. "Continuity, Conflict, and Change in Chile: A Study of the Pedagogic Projects of the Christian Democrat and the Popular Unity Governments." Ph.D. diss., University of London.

———, ed. 1985. *Hacia la Elaboración de Consensos en Política Educacional: Actas de una Discusión*. Santiago: CIDE.

———. 1991. "Sociedad y Conocimiento en Los 90s: Puntos para una Agenda Sobre Curriculum del Sistema Escolar." *FLACSO Documentos de Trabajo, Serie Educación y Cultura*, no. 11 (July).

———. 1993. "La politique de l'éducation du gouvernement de transition (1990–1994)." *Problèmes d'Amérique Latine: Numéro Spécial Chili* 11 (October–December).

———. 1997. *La Reforma de la Educación Chilena: Contexto, Contenidos, Implementación*. Santiago: PREAL.

Cuevas Farren, Gustavo, ed. 1993. *La Renovación Ideológica en Chile: Los Partidos y su Nueva Visión Estratégica*. Santiago: Universidad de Chile.

Cummings, William K., and Abby Riddell. 1993. "Alternative Policies for the Finance, Control, and Delivery of Basic Education." *International Journal for Educational Research* 17.

"Directiva Presidencial para la Educación." 1979. Santiago: mimeo.

"Educación Chilena: Información de Prensa No. 3: Directiva Presidencial Sobre Educación

Nacional, Carta al Ministro de Educación." March 5, 1979. Reproduced in José Vera Lamperein and Hernan Vera Lamperein, *La Municipalización de la Enseñanza.* Santiago: Editorial Andres Bello, 1982.

Edwards, Verónica, et al. *Directores y Maestros en la Escuela Municipalizada.* Santiago: Programa Interdisciplinario de Investigaciones en Educación, 1991.

"El Ladrillo": Bases de la Política Económica del Gobierno Military Chileno. 1992. Santiago: Centro de Estudios Públicos.

Elmore, Richard F. 1990. "Choice as an Instrument of Public Policy: Evidence from Education and Health Care." In William H. Clune and John F. Witte, eds., *Choice and Control in American Education,* Vol. 1: *The Theory of Choice and Control in Education.* New York: Falmer Press.

Elmore, Richard F., and Bruce Fuller. 1996. "Empirical Research on Educational Choice: What Are the Implications for Policy Makers?" In Bruce Fuller and Richard F. Elmore, eds., *Who Choses? Who Loses? Culture, Institutions, and the Unequal Effects of School Choice.* New York: Teachers College Press.

Espínola, Viola. 1993. "The Educational Reform of the Military Regime in Chile: The School System's Response to Competition, Choice, and Market Relations." Ph.D. diss., University of Wales, Cardiff College.

———. 1995. "The Decentralization of the Education System in Chile." Working paper. Santiago: CIDE.

Espinoza, Oscar, and Luis Eduardo González. 1993. *La Experiencia del Proceso de Desconcentración y Descentralización Educacional en Chile, 1974–1989.* Santiago: PIIE.

Farrell, Joseph. 1986. *The National Unified School in Allende's Chile: The Role of Education in the Destruction of a Revolution.* Vancouver: University of British Columbia Press.

Feigenbaum, Harvey B., and Jeffrey R. Henig. 1994. "The Political Underpinnings of Privatization: A Typology." *World Politics* 46 (January).

Fogg, S. L. 1978. "Positivism in Chile and its Impact on Educational Development and Economic Thought, 1870–1891." Ph.D. diss., New York University.

Friedman, Milton. 1955. "The Role of Government in Education." In Robert A. Solo, *Economics and the Public Interest.* New Brunswick, N.J.: Rutgers University Press.

———. 1962. "The Role of Government in Education." Chapter 6 of Friedman, *Capitalism in Freedom.* Chicago: University of Chicago Press.

Friedson, Eliot. 1986. *Professional Powers: A Study of the Institutionalization of Formal Knowledge.* Chicago: University of Chicago Press.

Frontaura Gómez, Juan. 1985. "Libertad de Enseñanza y Subvención." *Revista de Pedagogia* no. 283 (November).

Gajardo, Manuel. 1982. "Educación Chilena y Regimen Militar: Itinerario de Cambios." *FLACSO Documento de Trabajo No. 138.* Santiago: FLACSO.

González, Pablo. 1993. "Algunos Reflexiones en Torno al Vínculo entre Mercado Laboral y Educación." *Colleción de Estudios CIEPLAN* no. 37 (June).

Gormley, William T. 1991. *Privatization and Its Alternatives.* Madison: University of Wisconsin Press.

Graham, Carol. 1994. *Safety Nets, Politics, and the Poor: Transitions to Market Economies.* Washington, D.C.: Brookings Institution.

Gutmann, Amy. 1987. *Democratic Education.* Princeton: Princeton University Press.

Gysling, Jacqueline. 1992. *Profesores: Un Análisis de su Identidad Social.* Santiago: CIDE.

Haggard, Stephan. 1990. *Pathways from the Periphery: The Politics of Growth in the Newly Industrializing Countries*. Ithaca: Cornell University Press.

Hardin, Russell. 1982. *Collective Action*. Baltimore: Johns Hopkins University Press.

Hausmann, Ricardo. 1994. "Sustaining Reform: What Role for Social Policy?" In Colin I. Bradford, Jr., ed., *Redefining the State in Latin America*. Paris: OECD.

Henderson, V., et al. 1978. "Peer Group Effects and Educational Production Functions." *Journal of Public Economics* 10.

Henig, Jeffrey R. 1994. *Rethinking School Choice: The Limits of the Market Metaphor*. Princeton: Princeton University Press.

Hevia, Ricardo. 1982. *Cambios en la Administración Educacional: El Proceso de Municipalización*. Santiago: PIIE.

Hirschman, Albert O. 1970. *Exit, Voice, and Loyalty: Responses to Decline in Firms, Organizations, and States*. Cambridge: Harvard University Press.

Historia de Ley No. 19.070. 1992. Santiago: Biblioteca del Congreso Nacional.

Hochschild, Jennifer. 1984. *The New American Dilemma: Liberal Democracy and School Desegregation*. New Haven: Yale University Press.

Immergut, Ellen M. 1992. "The Rules of the Game: The Logic of Health Policy-Making in France, Switzerland, and Sweden." In Sven Steinmo et al., eds., *Structuring Politics: Historical Institutionalism in Comparative Analysis*. New York: Cambridge University Press.

Infante, María Teresa, and Ernesto Schiefelbein. 1992. "Asignación de Recursos Para la Educación Básica y Media: El Caso de Chile." Working paper. Santiago.

Isuani, Ernesto Aldo. 1994. "Social Policy and Political Dynamics in Latin America." In Stuart S. Nagel, ed., *Latin American Development and Public Policy*. New York: St. Martin's Press.

James, Estelle. 1987. "The Public/Private Division of Responsibility for Education: An International Comparison." *Economics of Education Review* 6 (1).

Jofré, Gerardo. 1988. "El Sistema de Subvenciones en Educación: La Experiencia Chilena." *Documento de Trabajo No. 99*. Santiago: Centro de Estudios Públicos.

Johnson, Daphne. 1990. *Parental Choice in Education*. London: Unwin Hyman.

Kliksberg, Bernardo. 1994. "Dilemmas and Solutions in the Implementation of Social Policies in Latin America." In Stuart S. Nagel, ed., *Latin American Development and Public Policy*. New York: St. Martin's Press.

Labarca H., Amanda. 1939. *Historia de le Enseñanza en Chile*. Santiago: Imprenta Universitaria.

Larrañaga, Osvaldo. 1994. "Politica Social en Chile durante la Transición a la Democracia: 1990–1993." *Serie Investigación Programa de Postgrado en Economia* 1 (78). Santiago: ILADES/Georgetown University.

Lavin, Sonia, and Doris Erlwein. 1993. *Autonomia, Gestión Escolar y Calidad de Educación: Estudio de Caso en Escuelas Municipalizadas y Particulares Subvencionadas en Chile*. Santiago: PIIE.

Letelier, Valentín. 1927. "Teoria de la Instrucción Pública," 1885. Reprinted in Valentín Letelier, *Filosofia de la Educación*. Buenos Aires: Cabaut y Companía.

Levin, Henry M. 1990. "The Theory of Choice Applied to Education." In William H. Clune and John F. Witte, eds., *Choice and Control in American Education, Volume 1: The Theory of Choice and Control in Education*. New York: Falmer Press.

Liberdad y Desarrollo. 1994. "Evolución de Sectores Sociales: Educación y Salud, 1990–1993." *Serre Opinión Social* 21, Santiago.

Lomnitz, Larissa, and Ana Melnick. 1991. *Chile's Middle Class: A Struggle for Survival in the Face of Neoliberalism.* Boulder: Lynne Rienner.

Lortie, Dan C. 1969. "The Balance of Control and Autonomy in Elementary School Teaching." In Amitai Etzioni, ed., *The Semi-Professions and Their Organization: Teachers, Nurses, Social Workers.* New York: Free Press.

Magendzo, Abraham, Loreto Egaña, and Carmen Luz Latorre. 1988. *La Educación Particular y los Esquemas Privatizantes en Educación bajo un Estado Subsidario (1973–1987).* Santiago: PIIE.

Marcel, Mario. 1993. "Descentralización y Desarrollo: La Experiencia Chilena." Paper presented at the Inter-American Development Bank conference, "En Route to Modern Growth," May 6.

Matte, Patricia, and Antonio Sancho. 1991. "Primary and Secondary Education." In Cristián Larroulet V., ed., *Private Solutions to Public Problems.* Santiago: Instituto Libertad y Desarrollo.

Medici, André Cesar, et al. 1997. "Managed Care and Managed Competition in Latin America and the Caribbean." In George Schieber, ed., *Innovations in Health Care Financing: Proceedings of a World Bank Conference, March 10–11, 1997.* Washington, D.C.: World Bank.

Ministerio de Educación. 1974. "Documento Normativo de Orientación General para la Segunda Semana de Actividades para-Académicas." Santiago: Ministerio de Educación.

———. 1992. *Compendio de Información Estadística: 1992.* Santiago: Ministerio de Educación.

———. 1994. "Dotación Docente." Santiago, mimeo.

Ministerio de Educación. Division de Planificación y Presupesto, 1994. "Dotación Docente y Gestión Municipal." Santiago.

Ministerio de Educación. Superintendencia de Educación. 1986. "Informe Sobre Déficits Municipales en Educación." Santiago, mimeo, July 18.

Ministerio de Hacienda. 1989. "Minuta: Comisión Análisis Financiero Educación Municipal." Reglamento 728, May 10.

Montero M., Enrique. 1980. "Discurso del Ministro Subsecretario del Interior, con motivo de los Congresos Regionales de Alcaldes," June–August. In Ministerio de Hacienda, Dirección de Presupesto, *Traspaso de Servicios Públicos a las Municipalidades: Manual de Consulta.* Santiago: Ministerio del Interior.

Montt L., Pedro, and Pedro Serra B. 1994. "La Descentralización Educativa en Chile: El Traspaso de la Educación a los Municipios." *ILPES Documento de Trabajo No. 3.* Santiago: CEPAL.

Murmane, Richard J., and David K. Cohen. 1986. "Merit Pay and the Evaluation Problem: Why Some Merit Pay Plans Fail and a Few Survive." *Harvard Educational Review* 56 (1).

Musgrave, R. 1959. *The Theory of Public Finance: A Study of the Public Economy.* New York: McGraw-Hill.

Núñez, Iván. 1984. *Las Transformaciones Educacionales Bajo el Regimen Militar.* Santiago: PIIE.

———. 1986. *Gremios del Magisterio: Setenta Años de Historia, 1900–1970.* Santiago: PIIE.

———. 1989. *La Reforma Educacional en Chile: 1940–1973*. Santiago: PIIE.

Oates, Wallace. 1972. *Fiscal Federalism*. New York: Harcourt Brace Jovanovich.

O'Donnell, Guillermo. 1994. "The State, Democratization, and Some Conceptual Problems." In William C. Smith, Carlos H. Acuña, and Eduardo A. Gamarra, eds., *Latin American Political Economy in the Age of Neoliberal Reform: Theoretical and Comparative Perspectives for the 1990s*. New Brunswick, N.J.: Transaction.

Olson, Mancur. 1965. *The Logic of Collective Action: Public Goods and the Theory of Groups*. Cambridge: Harvard University Press.

———. 1969. "The Principle of 'Fiscal Equivalence.'" *American Economic Review, Papers and Proceedings* 59 (May).

Osborne, David, and Ted Gaebler. 1992. *Reinventing Government: How the Entrepreneurial Spirit is Transforming the Public Sector*. New York: Penguin.

Ostrom, Elinor. 1990. *Governing the Commons: The Evolution of Institutions for Collective Action*. New York: Cambridge University Press.

Ostrom, Elinor, Larry Schroeder, and Susan Wynne. 1993. *Institutional Incentives and Sustainable Development: Infrastructure Policies in Perspective*. San Francisco: Westview Press.

Ostrom, Vincent, David Feeny, and Hartmut Picht. 1988. *Rethinking Institutional Analysis and Development: Issues, Alternatives, and Choices*. San Francisco: International Center for Economic Growth.

Ostrom, Vincent, and Elinor Ostrom. 1977. "Public Goods and Public Choices." In E. S. Savas, ed., *Alternatives for Delivering Public Services: Toward Improved Performance*. Boulder: Westview Press.

Parry, Taryn Rounds. 1993. "Theory Meets Reality in the Great Voucher Debate." Mimeo. University of Georgia.

———. 1994. "The Impact of Decentralization and Competition on the Quality of Education: An Assessment of Educational Reforms in Chile." Mimeo. University of Georgia.

Peterson, Paul E. 1981. *City Limits*. Chicago: University of Chicago Press.

———. 1990. "Monopoly and Competition in American Education." In William H. Clune and John F. Witte, eds., *Choice and Control in American Education, Volume 1: The Theory of Choice and Control in Education*. New York: Falmer Press.

El Pizarrón 40 (September–October 1986).

Politzer, Patricia. 1985. *Miedo en Chile*. Santiago: CESOC.

Prieto, Alfredo. 1983. *La Modernización Educacional*. Santiago: Ediciones Universidad Católica de Chile.

Puryear, Jeff. 1994. *Thinking Politics: Intellectuals and Democracy in Chile, 1973–1988*. Baltimore: Johns Hopkins University Press.

Raczynski, Dagmar, and Claudia Serrano. 1988. "Descentralización y Planificación Local: La Experiencia de Municipios en Comunas Pobres de Santiago." *CIEPLAN Notas Técnicas* 108 (January).

Rodríguez G., Jorge. 1988. "School Achievement and Decentralization Policy: The Chilean Case." *Revista de Análisis Económico* 3, no. 1 (June).

Rutter, Michael, et al. 1979. *Fifteen Thousand Hours: Secondary Schools and Their Effects on Children*. Cambridge: Harvard University Press.

Savas, E. S. 1987. *Privatization: The Key to Better Government*. Chatham, N.J.: Chatham House Publishers.

Schiefelbein, Ernesto. 1991. "Restructuring Education Through Economic Competition." *Journal of Educational Administration* 29, no. 4.

Schiefelbein, Ernesto, and Viterbo Apablazo, eds. 1984. *La Regionalización Educacional en Chile: ¿Municipalización o Alcaldización?* Santiago: CPU.

Shapiro, Carl, and Robert Willig. 1990. "Economic Rationales for the Scope of Privatization." In Ezra Suleiman and John Waterbury, eds., *The Political Economy of Public Sector Reform and Privatization.* Boulder: Westview Press.

Sigmund, Paul E. 1977. *The Overthrow of Allende and the Politics of Chile, 1964–1976.* Pittsburgh: University of Pittsburgh Press.

Sizer, Theodore R. 1984. *Horace's Compromise: The Dilemma of the American High School.* New York: Houghton Mifflin.

Smith, Adam. 1976. *An Inquiry into the Nature and Causes of the Wealth of Nations.* Chicago: University of Chicago Press.

Stein, Robert M. 1990. *Urban Alternatives: Public and Private Markets in the Provision of Local Services.* Pittsburgh: University of Pittsburgh Press.

Stiglitz, Joseph, et al. 1989. *The Economic Role of the State.* Oxford: Basil Blackwell.

Suleiman, Ezra N., and John Waterbury, eds. 1990. *The Political Economy of Public Sector Reform and Privatization.* Boulder: Westview Press.

Thelen, Kathleen, and Sven Steinmo. 1992. "Historical Institutionalism in Comparative Politics." In Steinmo et al., eds., *Structuring Politics: Historical Institutionalism in Comparative Analysis.* New York: Cambridge University Press.

Tiebout, Charles. 1956. "A Pure Theory of Local Expenditures." *Journal of Political Economy* 64.

Torres, Gerver, and Sarita Mathur. 1996. *The Third Wave of Privatization: Privatization of Social Sectors in Developing Countries.* Washington, D.C.: World Bank.

Touraine, Alan. 1994. "From the Mobilising State to Democratic Politics." In Colin I. Bradford, Jr., ed., *Redefining the State in Latin America.* Paris: OECD.

Tyack, David. 1974. *The One Best System: A History of American Public Education.* Cambridge: Harvard University Press.

Valenzuela, Arturo. 1977. *Political Brokers in Chile: Local Government in a Centralized Polity.* Durham: Duke University Press.

———. 1978. *The Breakdown of Democratic Regimes: Chile.* Baltimore: Johns Hopkins University Press.

Waggman, Craig. 1994. "'The End of History' and Neoliberalism in Latin America: A Concluding Essay." In Lowell S. Gustafson, ed., *Economic Development Under Democratic Regimes: Neoliberalism in Latin America.* Westport, Conn.: Praeger.

Walker, Ignacio. 1990. *Socialismo y Democracia: Chile y Europa en Perspectiva Comparada.* Santiago: Corporación de Investigación Económica para Latinoamerica.

Walzer, Michael. 1983. *Spheres of Justice: A Defense of Pluralism and Equality.* New York: Basic Books.

Williamson, John, ed. 1990. *Latin American Adjustment: How Much Has Happened?* Washington, D.C.: Institute for International Economics.

Winkler, Donald R., and Taryn Rounds. 1996. "Municipal and Private Sector Response to Decentralization and School Choice." *Economics of Education Review* 15.

Witte, John F. 1992. "Private School versus Public School Achievement: Are There Findings

That Should Affect the Educational Choice Debate?" *Economics of Education Review* 11, no. 4 (December).

Witte, John F., and Mark E. Rigdon. 1992. "Private School Choice: The Milwaukee Low-Income Voucher Experiment." Paper prepared for the 1992 meeting of the American Political Science Association, Chicago, September.

Witte, John F., and Christopher A. Thorn. 1996. "Who Chooses? Voucher and Interdistrict Choice Programs in Milwaukee." *American Journal of Education* 104 (May).

Witte, John F., et al. 1994. "Milwaukee Parental Choice Program: Fourth Year Report." Madison: Robert M. LaFollette Institute of Public Affairs, University of Wisconsin.

World Bank. 1992. *Chile: Subnational Government Finance*. Washington, D.C.: World Bank.

———. 1995. *Priorities and Strategies for Education: A World Bank Review*. Washington, D.C.: World Bank.

INDEX